PRAISE FOR

STIHL AMERICAN

"Crader's knack for keeping the story purely about real people, STIHL people, while detailing the business journey, including failures and heartwarming successes, made possible through hard work, grit, and risk, combined with American ingenuity and German engineering, is amazing. Having lived the experience along with most of the characters featured, I found the story a refreshing reminder of the hard work that laid the foundation for STIHL's American success."

—Rainer Glockle
Retired after forty-three active years with STIHL

"This is an insightful and informative story of the foundation and early beginnings of STIHL in the United States. Stan has done an admirable job of explaining the unique business approach to the market, the entrepreneurs and characters who ultimately and sometimes unwittingly implemented the long-term cultural success that was eventually spawned. All of this is accomplished with some personal historical insights and timely humor."

—Fred J. Whyte
Chairman of the Board
STIHL Incorporated

"Stan Crader's easy-reading book lays out the untold story of a number of independent small businessmen and entrepreneurs, whose hard work, honorable business dealings, and creative and positive thinking established a unique, cohesive, and highly successful national distribution system. Such was the basis for the successful, post-World War II reintroduction of the STIHL chainsaw to the United States. I look forward to a hoped-for sequel.

—John Williams
President of STIHL American, Inc. (1974–1975)
Son of STIHL American founder Gordon Williams

"There were a number of wonderful characters, some good businessmen, and a few strange ducks in the flock of distributors Gordon Williams had gathered together at STIHL American in the 1960s. Stan's own recollections of those days, coupled with his interviews with many of those early players, are a colorful snapshot of the beginnings of STIHL's successful expansion into America."

—Dorsey Glover
Founder Stihl Southwest

STIHL AMERICAN

Exemplary People—Extraordinary Times

Joe,

Finally !

A true story about

incredible people —

Stan Crader

Stan Crader

Stihl American: Exemplary People—Extraordinary Times

Published by Wheatmark®
2030 East Speedway Boulevard, Suite 106
Tucson, Arizona 85719 USA
www.wheatmark.com

ISBN: 978-1-62787-548-6
ISBN: 978-1-62787-549-3 (ebook)
LCCN: 2017950605

CONTENTS

PROLOGUE

ARTISTS BEGIN WITH A BLANK canvas and fill it with color to form an image. They create mosaics that they feel must be visually expressed.

Engineers see a need and their mind begins to design a remedy for fulfilling that need in a more efficient manner.

Authors begin with a blank sheet of paper. They fill the pages with prose that reveal a story that until told remains trapped inside.

All three have an insatiable urge to create something that will endure.

An artist's only limitation is their imagination and their God-given talent for expression. An engineer's limitation is their God-given intellect and skill for deductive reasoning, usually augmented by education. An author's story, the telling of an actual historical event, is limited on many fronts—memory, points of view, and available historical documents, just to name a few.

My goal with *Stihl American* is to respectfully profile a sampling of those responsible for STIHL's reintroduction to North America—but first, a confession. I was not able to find sufficient background on several significant players. At best, the work is incomplete, and at worst, the book falls miserably short of honoring all responsible for laying the foundation upon which so much success has been achieved. The information presented is based on my firsthand observations, stories told to me during recent interviews with others who also witnessed the reintroduction, magazine articles from the period represented, and the great work by Waldemar Schafer, *Stihl—From an Idea to a World Brand*.

It is my deepest desire that the following profiles are sufficiently representative to give the readers a good sense of the nature and tenacity of the real people who carved the path of success on the long and arduous journey that culminated in STIHL's manufacturing presence and market preeminence in America.

I have used my best judgment to tell the story with the essential facts intact.

This is my story. It is my memory and told from the heart.

Dedication

THEN CAME STIHL

WHILE CONTEMPLATING TO WHOM THIS work should be dedicated, it dawned on me that a story this splendid, about people whose lives affected so many, could not be limited to a single person. I've chosen three—Don Crader (my dad), Gordon Williams, and Andreas Stihl.

My STIHL experience was made possible by my dad, Don Crader — beginning with his initial decision to join my grandfather in the farm equipment business and continuing with his choice of STIHL to supplement the company's income. By coupling risk with hard work, he set the course that secured our family's financial future and that of many others for multiple generations. He unconsciously began teaching me business skills when, during town baseball games in which he played and was a great hitter, he set my sister and me up to sell sodas out of the back of his topless International Harvester Scout. I still have the belt-mounted coin changer from those heat-soaked days.

The tutoring began while I was in grade school and continued until the day of his death, fifty years later. I occasionally receive compliments regarding my business ethics. Although I graduated from the University of Missouri school of business, I learned all of the important stuff from my dad — who attended one year of college, and who learned his business ethics from my grandfather — who only completed eighth grade. Dad taught me to never stop learning, to understand that it's not what you know, but what you do with what you know that matters, and that people and relationships are the secret sauce to a business's enduring success.

Gordon Williams's first visit to Marble Hill to establish Crader Equipment as a STIHL Distributor is crystal clear in my mind's eye. Arriving in a Lincoln Continental with suicide doors, there was no doubt he was a man of means. Over the years I learned he was also a man of principle. His devotion to STIHL, the highest quality chainsaw on the market, and his commitment to the wholesale distribution strategy, eventually abandoned by nearly every other power equipment manufacturer, played a major role in STIHL's eventual market dominance. Gordon made possible the opportunity Dad gave me.

The genesis of STIHL's unparalleled success worldwide began with Andreas Stihl's invention of the one-man chainsaw. He first addressed the need to make work easier for woodcutters. His infamous trek across Canada set the example for salesmanship tenacity. Most of all, he assured the enduring success of STIHL by insisting on the maintenance of uncompromising manufacturing and customer service standards. I had the honor of first meeting Mr. Stihl in 1966, when he introduced the saw that truly set the course for STIHL's market dominance in America: the 040. The culture of product innovation, high-quality manufacturing standards, and aggressive marketing Mr. Stihl created has survived well into the third generation of the Stihl family.

His contribution is appropriately illustrated in the sculpture, "Then Came Stihl." The sculpture was commissioned by the Crader family and presented to the Stihl family as a token of recognition for the impact Stihl has made on our lives and the lives of many others.

Without Andreas Stihl, none of this would have happened.

Acknowledgments

THE SECRET SAUCE

I ENVY THOSE WHO PRODUCE works of nonfiction about which topics there are volumes of reference material available in libraries, magazines, and periodicals. The story of STIHL's reintroduction to North America is about people who were consumed with meeting the challenges one day at a time. They weren't the journal-keeping variety, and any records that were kept are now long gone or tucked away in a dusty box in a seldom-used section of a storage facility, never to be found. The STIHL American story was only possible due to the many who shared their memories, photographs, and supporting documents. The following are those who made significant contributions.

All the records pertaining to Central Equipment were consumed in a home fire. Stan Banks, the son of Jack Banks, took the time to reconstruct, from memory, the history of Central Equipment.

Cheri Belander's assistance with the details about her father was essential while writing the profile on Virg Hatfield.

Paul Bobeen's family has been a STIHL dealer for five decades. It was only through his contribution that the story of one of STIHL's oldest dealers was possible.

My wife, Debbie, and I had the pleasure of meeting with Hugo and Rita Brandt in their home in Lynn, Missouri. They're both up there in years, but their memories were crisp. They shared many memories and a few precious 1920s photographs, including one from when Charles Lindbergh paid the Lynn area a visit.

Rick Bryan III provided several hours of recorded history of the Bryan family, including their relation to Daniel Boone.

Gene Coakley provided a video of an interview with Bill Warren and additional notes regarding the history of STIHL Northwest.

I found Christine Ross Everett on Facebook, and she provided me with the interesting and unique details of her parents, Tom and Margo Reck.

Dan Feldman filled me in on the history of Feldman's, a long-time exclusive STIHL dealer and member of the Wheatbelt Association, many members of which are excellent STIHL dealers.

Bob Gillespie, of Titan Chainsaw fame, provided the photo of a young Fred Whyte making his first cut with a chainsaw.

Without the help of Rainer Gloeckle, this book would not have been possible. He and I spoke several times by phone to discuss the people and details of STIHL American. Rainer provided many of the photographs.

Dorsey and Elaine Glover invited my wife and me for a weekend in their beautiful Arkansas lakeside home to discuss the story. Dorsey's memory is second to none, and as an attorney he keeps copious records. His daughter, Susan Brittain, was also a big help, especially with photographs.

Reinhold Guhl's granddaughter, Isabella Guhl, found the story about Reinhold on my blogsite, read it to Reinhold, and confirmed the story of the famous speech. I was thrilled to learn that Reinhold was alive and well. I hope to personally deliver a copy of the book to him.

One of the most fun parts of research for this book was meeting

Jimmy and Barb Hampton near their home in New Hampshire at the Mt. Washington Resort. Staying at the resort was a blast, but spending the day with Jimmy and learning his story was an absolute privilege.

It was during a lunch with my wife, Debbie, and STIHL Inc.'s VP, Nick Jiannis, and his wife, Cristina, at a STIHL meeting in Sedona, Arizona, that I made the commitment to write the book. Nick and Cristina's encouragement was the final straw. Cristina's follow-up inquiry about the book was encouraging.

I'd known Kenny Johnson since he started with STIHL American. Once he heard I was working on the history of STIHL American, he began sending me copies of articles, magazines, old STIHL accessories, and anything that he thought would help. Kenny passed away during the course of the writing. His son, Dana, was kind enough to provide additional details that I'd failed to get from Kenny.

Another pure delight during the book's research took me to the home of Joe and Evelyn Minarik on Massachusetts's beautiful Cape Cod. By the time I made it to Joe, he'd been suffering from cancer and didn't have long to live. His body was weak, but his was memory clear and vivid. We visited for the better part of a day. A week or so after the visit, he sent me a beautifully handwritten letter thanking me for the visit and including several details he'd failed to mention during our precious time together. He and his wife were jewels.

Francee McClain, the assistant to Crader Distributing's marketing director, came to our scanner's rescue several times. She seemed to be able to sense when I'd reached my wit's end trying to scan photos and was about to take the office scanner to the parking lot, fill it with Tannerite, and blow it to smithereens. Several times she instructed me to return to my office. While dreaming of all kinds of ways to destroy the stubborn scanner, the photos I'd sweated over would appear as JPEG files in emails from Francee.

Outdoor Power Equipment (OPE) editor, Steve Noe, included excerpts of the book in multiple editions of *OPE*, helping promote the book and preserving the story.

Heidi Poel, one of the most patriotic Americans I know, immigrated to the United States in the 1960s. I asked her to edit the story from the perspective of someone who knew very little about STIHL products or STIHL American. Her edit was thorough, and her comments helped provide a better story, especially for readers not in the power equipment business. Most interesting was the discovery that she'd sailed to the United States on the same ship on which Kenny Johnson had served while in the navy during World War II. Also interesting was that her childhood home was the same area in Germany where the namesake for Herman, Missouri, had gained fame.

Many of the photos included in the book are from STIHL's website. Dave Ross provided high-resolution copies of each.

Niko Stihl provided a copy of the extraordinary letter from Arthur Mall to his grandfather acknowledging the copying of STIHL's patents by American manufacturers.

Dan Shell of Hatton-Brown publishing, owners of *Chain Saw Age (CSA)* graciously agreed to allow photos to be scanned from *CSA* magazines and promoted STIHL American in *Power Equipment Trade*.

Wayne Sutton is a bit of a STIHL historian himself. He and I had several valuable conversations during the course of this project.

Jerry Swisher provided the photo of America's first zero-turn mower, which was designed by his father, Ray Swisher.

Bob Van Schelven knew the Williams family long before he began working at STIHL American. His insight was most valuable.

Fred Whitson attended his first STIHL distributor meeting along with me in 1966. His memory and respect for STIHL's early days is remarkable. Fred's contribution of details and copies of magazines was very helpful.

Udo Wagner began at STIHL Parts and ended his career with STIHL as VP of marketing worldwide. His knowledge of STIHL and STIHL American is a treasure.

Fred Whyte and I met at his home during the last few days of his battle with cancer. Fred assured me that I'd told the story as it needed to be told. I hope he was right.

Without the help of John and Craig Williams, this story would be miserably incomplete and have many important details missing. The two of them provided photographs, magazine articles, and hours of narrative filling in the personal history of their father, Gordon, and their father's friend Harding. Their sister, Liz, was a source of confirmation and encouragement to keep writing.

John Woody, Jr. helped with the early history of STIHL in America's Southeast.

Jim Zuidema, the last person to retire from STIHL Inc., who'd also been employed at STIHL Parts during the STIHL American era, provided essential information about the early days and also did a first edit. It's people like Jim who exude the STIHL culture, which makes all the difference.

Last but not least, I thank my wife, Debbie, for putting up with my zoned-out looks when I was mentally working out details of the book or fretting over a historical gap. This has been an arduous three-year project that has included travel, research, writing, editing, and rewriting. Just before sending the manuscript to the publisher, she read it aloud while I listened. During the grueling three-day process, we rooted out repetitive adjectives, eliminated unnecessary adverbs, scrubbed the many split infinitives and dangling prepositions, and made the work better. It was her idea to use the photo for the cover.

The story of STIHL's reintroduction to the United States is told with great respect. Details and events are told with as much accuracy as memory and scant record-keeping could provide. Some scenes are depicted based on outcomes and may not be precise representations. It's the essence of the people that's important for the reader to grasp.

Chapter One

SEE SOMETHING, SAY SOMETHING

STIHL SAWS WERE ORIGINALLY INTRODUCED and sold in the United States in the 1930s. A gentleman, who would later become one of STIHL's largest distributors, sold one of those first STIHLs. During World War II, STIHL lost all patent protection in the United States, sales of STIHL in the United States ceased, and several American manufacturers immediately copied STIHL's patents. Nearly two decades passed before the world's leading brand of chainsaw would be reintroduced to the world's biggest market.

The notion of writing a book about STIHL's reintroduction to the United States and the pioneers who first scoured the country-side in search of dealers willing to represent the German-made chainsaw haunted me for nearly a decade.

When speaking to people about responsibility, I like to convert the phrase "somebody ought to do something about this sometime" to "I need to do something about this now." Advice is always easier to give than receive. Regrettably, I waited too long to follow my own advice.

"You should write a book." That's what I tell people when they relentlessly harp on and on about a subject that's obviously important to them and pertains to something they fear few know, but should. Evidently, my repeated comments about the mostly forgotten first slate of STIHL distributors in America, combined with me being one of the few people who has been around since STIHL's reintroduction to the United States and is still associated with STIHL, plus the fact that I have written a few books, apparently qualified me as the STIHL American historian—at least by those urging me to take my own advice. Ugh . . . the tables had clearly turned.

It's generally easy to know the right decision; however, it's the full realization of the consequence of a difficult decision that causes making the decision to be challenging. I'd reached the conclusion that the story needed to be told but couldn't bring myself to personally accept the responsibility for doing so and ultimately make the commitment until attending my second STIHL fortieth anniversary celebration. I'd attended my first STIHL fortieth-anniversary event nearly fifty years earlier.

This most recent fortieth, October 2014, was celebrating the fortieth anniversary of the 1974 plant opening in Virginia Beach. It was a splendid affair held in Virginia Beach's massive convention center. One area was cleverly set up displaying memorabilia typical of 1974. Seeing a manual typewriter, adding machine, rotary dial telephone, and other now obsolete items was a first for many in attendance, many of whom weren't yet born by 1974.

Standing in the massive convention hall, surrounded by over two thousand people, I felt suffocated and eerily alone. The shortness of breath was induced by hearing too many comments about the remarkable success of STIHL in the US since 1974, particularly from those who sincerely believed that STIHL's American experience had begun only forty years earlier, in Virginia Beach. The paradoxical feeling of being alone while standing in the midst of thousands had washed over me once I realized that, other than Peter Stihl, and a scant few others, I was the only person in attendance who had witnessed the original reintroduction of STIHL to America, which had occurred well before the establishment of the manufacturing plant in Virginia Beach. Overwhelmed with emotion, I reached this conclusion: I needed to do something about this misconception now—*this* being the rest of the story of STIHL in America. Looking around, it was clear that a great deal is known of STIHL's American experience since 1974; my focus would be on the forgotten era. I looked around while pondering how best to tell the story. I'd seen and now I needed to say.

My momentary funk was interrupted when I spotted the then first lady of STIHL in America, Karen Whyte. Her husband, Fred Whyte, had joined STIHL American immediately following college and had spent his entire working career with STIHL, culminating in his long tenure as president. Judging by her expression, she was as lost in the vast sea of people as I was. She smiled relief and headed my way after we made eye contact. "Have you seen Fred?" she asked.

I'd just seen Fred and pointed toward the front of the convention center to a group of suited men who surrounded him—a typical occurrence for the president of STIHL, the leading outdoor power tool company in America. "He's right over there," I said.

"I hate to interrupt him," Karen said, "but I need to know where he parked the car."

"Nonsense," I said, and walked her through the crowd to find out where Fred had parked the car. Fred was gracious, as always. The suits dispersed, and I observed Fred and Karen having a private husband and wife moment in spite of being surrounded by thousands of jubilant celebrants.

It was a short but powerful moment. I'd been unable to make the commitment to write a book about STIHL American due to my inability to decide how to tell the story. Seeing and speaking to Karen crystalized the solution. Knowing Fred's history, the unique way in which Fred and Karen had met at the University of Iowa, and the tie that Fred represented between the old and new guard caused me to realize the story would be about the people, with STIHL being the binding tie.

I deeply wish I'd decided to embark on the project a year sooner. My father, Don Crader, a STIHL distributor since 1960, had passed away earlier that year—February 2014. While he remains a golden source of inspiration, gone with him—along many other STIHL pioneers—is an invaluable source of information. My mother's passing was the primary driving force to my series of novels; my father's memory is the driving force for my first non-fiction: *Stihl American*.

Good stories have a strong, recognizable beginning, middle, and end. The beginning of the STIHL American story is the birth of Andreas Stihl; the middle is the primary subject of the book: STIHL's reintroduction in America. The end of the STIHL story is yet to be and is not likely to occur anytime soon.

During the course of the story, the reader will note that two entities are mentioned for the period covered—STIHL American and STIHL Parts. While the two entities operated mutually exclusively in terms of ownership and management, they were mutually beneficial, with common customers, highly coordinated in terms of business and product needs, and with the gains of each benefiting the other. For practical purposes, references to STIHL American include STIHL Parts.

All the early players, including STIHL American, were small businesses, totally consumed with scratching out a miniscule profit while raising families; few kept adequate records, and most records kept are no longer available. Digital photography had yet to be invented, good cameras were cumbersome, and photographs expensive; so, photographs of the pioneers are few, and those that survived are generally of poor quality. Most of the key individuals are deceased, and consequently, much of the information collected was indirect word-of-mouth. The following is from my memory and that of others. All stories are told with an inevitable bias, and great stories are told in a unique way. This story is no different.

Much of the story will be cloaked in a 1966 trip to Germany on which, at the age of ten, I had the extraordinary honor of tagging along.

I saw something incredible, and now I'm saying something.

Chapter Two

IT'S A SWISS NAME

EARLY ONE FROSTY FALL MORNING in the mid-eighties, I was standing outside the locked front door of a STIHL dealer in Scottsbluff, Nebraska. Since I'd failed to change my watch from central to mountain, I'd arrived an hour before they opened. While waiting, a small elderly gentleman on a morning walk strolled up and, after noticing the STIHL logo on my jacket, announced, "STIHL, it's a Swiss name." His English was crystal clear, but he spoke with an accent.

I knowingly replied, "No, it's German."

The gentleman stopped, spun confidently toward me, and responded, "No, it's Swiss."

After introducing myself, I politely explained to Mr. Aluisius that I knew the Stihl family personally, had met them on several occasions, and that they were most assuredly German. He would have none of it and then shared his unique story.

His was an interesting and, at times, moving story in which I learned that after a forced evacuation from his home in Lithuania, most of his family had fled to Russia, but he'd chosen Germany. He'd later joined the German army where he'd primarily served guarding Americans at a war prison. He wasn't outwardly proud or boastful of his wartime service but didn't seem to be ashamed either. After the war, while on trial for war crimes, the judge in his trial had coincidentally—or I prefer, providentially—been a prisoner of war under Mr. Aluisius's watch. The judge, remembering and noting Mr. Aluisius's kind treatment, granted him his freedom and asylum in America. Mr. Aluisius began work on a farm in central Nebraska and claimed he eventually became chief of police in Scottsbluff.

Intrigued and somewhat taken by his story, and thinking I might send him a note, I asked for his address. He gave me his but didn't ask for mine. We parted ways, each being sure the other was wrong. Less than a year later, I had the privilege of having dinner with Mr. Hans Peter Stihl and shared with him the story the Lithuanian from Nebraska told me. Peter settled the dispute.

Without an inkling of doubt, the reintroduction of STIHL into the American market would not be possible without Andreas Stihl, the father of the chainsaw, the Stihl family, ANDREAS STIHL AG & Co., and of course, STIHL products. While STIHL is the common thread in the stories that follow, respectfully, STIHL is not the focus. STIHL in the United States will feature the people who, with the critical support of STIHL, established the foundation for what is now STIHL's most valuable market. There was a great degree of variety among the eclectic group of men and women who drove the strategies most appropriate for the numerous unique markets in the vast and diverse expanse that was and is America.

Keeping in mind that the reintroduction of STIHL in the United States and the focus of the following began in 1958, the purist will no doubt claim the true beginning to be the birth of Andreas Stihl, in Zurich, Switzerland; Mr. Aluisius was right. I wrote Mr. Aluisius a note and let him know; he never wrote back, but he did show the note to the local dealer.

Chapter Three

PATIENT PERSISTENCE — PROGRESS

MOST AMERICANS ARE TAUGHT TO recall the 1930s as a dreadful time in American history; it was quite the opposite with STIHL. Andreas made his famous journey crisscrossing Canada during the 1930s to personally demonstrate his revolutionary product to North America.

Five hundred miles to the south, a trio of Ridgewood, New Jersey, high school classmates formed a friendship that would last a lifetime and would include instrumental roles in STIHL's re-introduction in America.

Near Chicago a young descendant of Daniel Boone's sister would sell one of the first STIHLs in the United States while working for Mall Tool Company.

In Arkansas, a lawyer's wife would give birth to a future counselor who'd sell STIHL for over fifty years. In Saint Louis, a tire repair station owner's wife would give birth to a piano player whose company would eventually grow into one of STIHL's largest customers worldwide.

A young couple in Ohio gave birth to a son who'd establish STIHL in the high plains, while another Ohio couple gave birth to a baseball player who'd eventually be recruited by baseball's legendary Eddie Stanky — but who'd ultimately choose a career with STIHL instead of playing professional baseball.

A young beauty from Missouri, while attending Smith Girl's college, would marry a Harvard MBA and drag him to her Missouri hometown where he'd later become a STIHL distributor.

Possibly most astounding, after rescuing him from Oklahoma's Osage Indian Reservation in the 1920s, a devoted couple in Colorado continued, into the 1930s, raising a young Osage Indian who'd lost his parents in the midst of the Osage Indian Reservation murder-for-oil tragedy.

A Hatfield boy—descendent of the Appalachian Hatfield/McCoy Feud fame—stood in an Oregon Cascade mountain meadow and watched a barnstormer perform, longed to fly, and would eventually use a small plane to make dealer and end-user calls throughout the Northwest.

Just as with a giant, magnificent oak, enduring roots require years to develop before the massive edifice takes shape and is noticed. So it was with STIHL.

Recently, numerous companies, particularly dot-com enterprises, have been founded on a shoestring, enjoyed overnight success, and zoomed to record-breaking unparalleled market capitalization levels, and in some cases, their CEOs were assigned celebrity status. In many cases the inflated values are based more on concept than developed product. Popular, present-day business practices include high-risk strategies with the goal of rapid market penetration, acquiring competitors, positioning the company to be sold, and using—rather than serving—the customer.

Most contemporary companies have little interest in vertical channel integration and participation; company goals are centered on meeting financial analysts' whimsical, spreadsheet-driven expectations first and customer service second, if at all. For most companies the roots are nonexistent or very shallow, which explains their demise at the first financial setback—not so with STIHL.

STIHL's journey to success is more traditional, taking nearly an entire generation before the company hit its stride and began the journey to market domination. STIHL's secret to success—intense total channel participation from raw material through the life of the product, including while in the hands of the end user—is made possible because the company is, and has always been, privately held. While profit is the goal, the STIHL strategy does not include meeting quirky quarterly market expectations; the STIHL strategy is patient persistence.

STIHL's highest expectations begin with the product, which bears its highly respected family name. STIHL's reintroduction to the United States coincided with a time when so many giant corporations were consumed with process and organizational structure. One need look no further than the American automotive industry of the 1960s and 1970s to see the result of too much focus on process and not enough on product quality. STIHL, much like the then foreign automobile manufacturers, understood that product quality trumped organizational process. Product quality remains the preeminent focal point at STIHL.

Equally essential are channel relations, including the end user. Market expansion ideas are discussed only after product quality and channel relations are assured. STIHL's dedication to channel partners and customer service is without equal. STIHL began with an idea for a product focused on a single application; STIHL has now been number one in their class for several years. As they say, "time will tell." Well, time has told, and STIHL's strategy has endured wars, changing market conditions, cultural swings, and multiple generations of management by family members—no easy task.

Just as Mr. Aluisius had told me on the empty early morning street in Nebraska, the history of STIHL in the United States began in Switzerland. The story begins to take shape in 1926, with providential seeds propagated during the 1930s, but wouldn't begin to brilliantly bloom for another twenty years: patient persistence— progress.

Chapter Four

STIHL TAKES FLIGHT

OSTENSIBLY PROVIDENTIAL, WHILE A PERSONAL commitment to my late father and the STIHL American pioneers began during a STIHL fortieth anniversary, the first STIHL distributor meeting I attended, along with STIHL American forerunners—nearly fifty years earlier—was likewise a fortieth anniversary, celebrating STIHL's auspicious 1926 beginning.

Just before dinner one night in the fall of 1965, Mom and Dad were whispering; that was seldom good. "We have something we need to tell you." They promised to tell my sister, Teri, and me the big secret during dinner.

"Pregnant again?" Teri asked. Mom ignored her, and together they delivered the news, each interrupting the other when the news wasn't progressing fast enough for the other. I didn't hear much of anything else that was said after Dad told us that STIHL had chartered a private jet to fly from New York to Germany. My sister had the same reaction after Mom mentioned the trip included Paris, France. They talked about Paris while Dad and I discussed more important matters: transatlantic night flights and intercontinental navigation. Dad had been learning German from the town doctor who lived across the street in a small apartment with his wife. They were both foreign and strange, and they had an annoying, talking myna bird, which spent most days in a cage on their screened-in porch, for the miserable benefit of neighbors.

Teri and I always washed dishes after dinner while Mom sat on the porch sipping her coffee, enjoying a Pall Mall, and Dad played the piano—Strauss's "Blue Danube." The dishes, usually a dreaded drudgery, weren't a problem that night.

In January 1966, 144 STIHL American distributor personnel were treated to a week in Germany as guests of STIHL American and the Stihl family in celebration of the fortieth anniversary of the founding of STIHL Maschinenfabrik by Andreas Stihl. Thanks to my dad, and the graciousness of STIHL American, Teri and I were among the fortunate 144.

Since Saint Louis was TWA's main hub, it appeared that TWA was the only airline serving Saint Louis, even though Ozark Airlines had nearly as many daily flights. TWA's giant red logo was mounted behind the multistory, curvaceously arched windows of Saint Louis Lambert Field's main terminal. Interestingly, Lambert's main terminal had been designed by Architect Minoru Yamasaki, who would design other American airports, including JFK International, and eventually the World Trade Center.

The flight from Saint Louis to New York aboard a Boeing 727 was my introductory commercial flight. TWA was easy enough to figure out—Trans World Airlines. Since my dad was taking flying lessons, I'd survived several private-plane rides, read his ground school book, and was a self-declared expert on the subject of flight and navigation. Few people know more than that which dwells in the overactive imagination of a precocious ten-year-old. Boarding the 727 offered more new experience than I was able to quickly absorb, filling my sensory nodes to capacity. After taking a window seat, I looked at the wings and verified the round contour of the leading edge as depicted in the wing-chord section of the Cessna ground school manual. While wondering how much the behemoth weighed, it dawned on me that I had no idea who the pilot was and, of a more serious nature, had no verification of his qualification. Nobody else seemed too concerned, so I succumbed to group ignorance and complacency. The roar of the engines and the transition from a bumpy, fast taxi to a smooth, quiet, airborne ride filled me with wonderment and post-anxiety drowsiness. I'm not sure when I lost consciousness, but during our approach to New York International Dad elbowed me awake in time to see the Statue of Liberty and the densely packed sky scrapers of New York City off in the distance.

I'd used our new set of encyclopedias to look up the population of New York City, Germany, France, and Paris—places we'd be visiting. New York had roughly ten times more people than Saint Louis; from the sky, while on approach, the Big Apple looked twenty times bigger. Walking through the terminal on the way to our departing gate, there were more airline company signs than I could count. Most I'd never heard of, but then, I'd only heard of two—TWA and Ozark—and Ozark was nowhere to be found in New York.

Unbearably anxious to see the private chartered jet that was to take all of us to Germany, I kept running ahead and getting called back. I was vaguely familiar with the concept of charter flights—a flight in which a high roller rents a small four- or six-passenger airplane and hires a pilot to fly him somewhere, usually a business meeting. The concept and purpose of business meetings had yet to register in my formative ten-year-old brain, but if it involved flying, I was interested in learning.

Imagine my unbridled eagerness when we reached the gate for the Germany-bound flight and I set eyes on our chartered jet—a four-engine behemoth, the largest airplane I'd ever seen. KLM was emblazoned in giant blue letters on the STIHL chartered plane, and in smaller font: Royal Dutch Airlines. I was immediately suspicious, curious, and exponentially overwhelmed. For starters—how did they get Royal Dutch Airlines out of KLM? Having seen the tickets, I knew the initials, but I expected—as with TWA—that they'd represent something sensible. The KLM mystery momentarily took second fiddle while I looked at the giant engines, tried to imagine how a turbine worked as opposed to a piston engine, and wondered how much fuel it would take to reach Germany. It was too much for a ten-year-old to contemplate. The gate area began to fill with STIHL people from all over America, the men wearing ties and the ladies dresses; that's how people dressed when they traveled back then. To this day, I wear a tie when traveling to New York. I don't have to, but I do so voluntarily, which makes it more fun. On that day in 1966, I was wearing a herringbone fedora, an overcoat, and my best clip-on tie.

International Hat Company had a factory in Marble Hill, and they regularly sold seconds for fifty cents. I had a collection of hats with barely noticeable flaws and had chosen the best for the trip. In anticipation of the Germany trip, I'd gotten a black overcoat for Christmas. It was the kind with a thick zip-out lining. So, sporting the overcoat, fedora, and tie, I felt at home among the adults. There were a few other kids in the crowd, but I avoided them, thinking they didn't know any more than I knew. I had a lot of questions: solving the KLM Royal Dutch business, navigation, and fuel flow.

Gordon and Ann Williams had arrived first and were greeting everyone as soon as they reached the waiting area. While shaking hands, Gordon said he was glad I was able to make the trip, and I was certain he'd meant it. His egalitarian disposition was natural and engaging. I'd given him my best shoulder-dislodging handshake, to no avail. A man who had to be the Osage Indian chief that Dad had promised I'd meet arrived: Chief Beatty, the distributor based in Denver, Colorado. I watched him introduce his wife to Ann, Gordon's wife. The two women smiled and dipped their chins slightly, which I'd often observed ladies do when they couldn't think of anything pertinent to say. Most of the men had met, but it was a first for the wives. There was a lot of chin dipping going on while the crowd gathered.

I spotted Ernie Rainey. I'd met him when he and Gordon Williams had visited Marble Hill in their Lincoln Continental with the suicide doors—a first for Marble Hill—but I'd never met his wife, the former Miss New Hampshire. I spotted a striking blond-haired lady that was surely she. A gaggle of chin dippers had lined up to meet her as well.

"There she is," Dad said, and discretely pointed in the direction of a tall, athletic-looking lady standing with a man wearing a hat similar to mine, but probably one for which he'd paid full price. Dad had just finished telling me about the wife of the STIHL distributor in Saint Joe, Missouri. She'd flown bombers in World War II.

After we posed for a group photo in which I was asked to help hold a giant sign that read *Heppy Gewinn*, probably because of my fedora and 007 overcoat, we began to board. Most, no doubt, thought *Heppy Gewinn* was the German spelling for "happy going," but it was actually an inside joke. Gordon's nickname for his daughter, Liz, was Heppy, which was short for Hepzibah, who Gordon claimed was the mother of Peter Rabbit. When first born, Liz had reminded Gordon of a tiny bunny. *Gewinn*, translated, means "profit" or "win." No matter one's interpretation, the sign worked, and most important for Gordon, made Liz especially happy.

The captain and a stewardess were greeting each passenger and pointing each person in the direction of his or her assigned seat. Since mine was in the rear of the plane, I was among the first to board. I ignored the stewardess and asked the captain what KLM stood for. He replied, *Koninklijke Luchtvaart Maatschappij.* Royal Dutch Airlines (KLM) was the world's oldest airline then, and remains so today.

Prior to the trip, I'd learned a few German words and phrases when delivering the newspaper to the doctor's foreign wife — words such as *danke, bitte, guten morgen, wo ist dos fruhstuck, auf wiedersehen,* and most important, *wo ist die toilette.* I admit no recollection of precisely what the captain said, only the sensation of nearly swallowing my tongue while trying to repeat the words and commit them to memory. It was probably then and there that I decided foreign language wasn't to be my strong suit. Years later — well over fifty years later — I googled KLM and determined what the captain must have said. At the time, I smiled as if I'd understood precisely, replied, *danke,* and then changed the subject to something about which I thought I knew by asking how ocean-crossing navigation worked since there couldn't possibly be ground-based navigation aids in the middle of the deep blue sea. It was a question my dad couldn't answer, and I was hoping the captain knew. I was expecting a lesson on how to use a sextant.

The captain smiled knowingly and patted me on the shoulder. "He can answer all of your questions," he said, and pointed me toward the copilot. My dad always directed me to my mom when I asked him a question he didn't know. The captain was probably doing the same. The copilot was glancing around the cockpit and making checkmarks on what I recognized from Dad's ground school book had to be a checklist—a giant one, possibly the mother of all checklists. While the rest of the fortunate 144 made their way down the aisle, the copilot explained several of the gauges, confirmed I knew how a VOR worked, explained great circle and inertia navigation, and why the route from New York to Stuttgart looked like a curved line on a flat paper map. I stopped paying attention to the lesson on navigation when he began explaining the Coriolis Effect and how the velocity and direction of wind changes more drastically as flights near the Arctic Circle.

I was happy to learn that the plane was manufactured by McDonnell Douglas, with a factory in Saint Louis, rather than Boeing, with a factory in who knows where. Even though I offered to sit in the tiny jump seat across from the flight engineer and help with weight and balance, the captain—probably noticing I'd learned all I could in one visit—suggested I find my seat. However, he promised I could return after dinner had been served. Dinner sounded good, so I headed toward the rear of the gigantic chartered jet.

Between the cockpit, galley, and the passenger section was a small table surrounded on three sides by a padded bench. Nobody was seated there during takeoff, but soon thereafter, a group from STIHL American would gather and began toasting to the success manifested by the flight to STIHL's headquarters and factory in Germany. To the uninformed, the toasts represented what had occurred since 1958; they would be shortsighted. While STIHL American was less than five years old and the reintroduction of STIHL in the United States had officially begun in 1958, the story of STIHL began long before that, long before flight itself, and just as Mr. Aluisius tried to explain, the beginning hadn't occurred in Germany.

Chapter Five

GENIUS REVEALED

SINCE I'D BE MISSING A week of school while on the trip, I was required to do a report on STIHL and my experience during the trip. I have no memory of that paper except that I was required to do it. Teri had a similar assignment but a different teacher; it's possible that I copied hers. If I were doing a paper on STIHL today, it would begin in the following way.

Imagine Maria in the Sound of Music, played by Julie Andrews, sprinting across a lush Alpine mountainside, singing "The Sound of Music." Selina von Wertmuller, like Maria, was an Alpine orphan. Unlike Maria, Selina didn't marry a wealthy man and move to America. Selina married a young German trucker, Andreas, and they founded a small trucking company in Zurich, Switzerland, during the mid-1890s. Bear in mind, Gottlieb

Daimler didn't develop the first general-purpose flatbed truck or motorized cart until 1896, so the STIHL trucking company was probably something less than what comes to mind today when one thinks about a trucking company.

On November 10, 1896, Selina gave birth to a boy; they named him Andreas, after the father. After finishing primary school, young Andreas moved to Germany and lived with extended family while attending grammar and secondary school. Andreas earned a degree in mechanical engineering and was subsequently employed by firms providing steam engines for sawmills. It has been said that need is the mother of invention, and Andreas saw and experienced the need for better timber-harvesting tools—particularly a portable saw, to make work easier and more efficient in the timber industry.

Andreas Stihl first attempted a partnership with a friend and fellow engineer. The short-lived partnership was dissolved in 1926. Andreas, not dissuaded by the lack of success with a partner, formed a sole proprietorship—A. STIHL Engineering Consultancy—and developed the first portable tree-felling machine the same year. 1926 is the year of the promising event that would initially have minimal impact on Bavarian timber harvesting but would eventually become a true paradigm-shattering occurrence worldwide. Officially, the first patent wasn't registered until 1928, but the promising beginning of the real STIHL story took irrepressible root in 1926. The saying of the day became "the saw was taken to the wood rather than the wood to the saw." It was then that the genius of STIHL was first revealed.

"Portable" is a relative term. Portable in those days simply meant the device was not permanently attached or not designed to be moved. The first gasoline-powered chainsaw that might conceivably be considered portable in today's terms wasn't produced until 1929.

Andreas's first hire was Alwin Fauser, who remained with the company until retirement several decades later. One by one, Fauser was joined by countless others, dedicated to superior product development.

Andreas Stihl exuded high standards and expected no less from those he chose to join his budding company. He hired only highly competent, diligent workers whom he trusted and respected. In spite of occasional fits of rage brought on by an inventor's frustration—such as when he'd fire the top echelon in the company and then hire them back within days—he ultimately earned the unconditional trust and respect of all and became the inspiration for thousands, then and now.

In a 1976 speech given at a STIHL Distributor gathering in Phoenix, Arizona, Eva Mayr Stihl said the following about her late father, Andreas Stihl: "In 1926 my father stood at the very beginning of his work, and first, a company had to be established. He did this in the same year, with only one coworker and a great deal of trust in the Lord. The first saws built had electric motors. Fortunately, they could be sold quickly, which provided the new company with the necessary funds for continuing the development of a portable saw for the woodcutter."

Whereas, the first felling machine was produced in 1926, the first portable gasoline-powered saw wasn't introduced until 1929. *Portable* should not be confused with *light*; the first portable saw required at least two stout Bavarians to move it from tree to tree. What would be thought of as heavy by today's standards was considered conveniently light in 1929.

STIHL saws were sold as quickly as they could be produced. Looking forward to the 1930 trade fair in Leipzig, Andreas—a marketer as well as an inventor—decided it appropriate to develop a company logo: the stump. He hired STIHL's twenty-fifth employee that year.

Outwardly, Andreas was a quintessential, laconic, Swiss-born German, but there's ample evidence of a soft heart. First, he was always accompanied by a dog, usually a German boxer. Legend has it that the only time the boxer (Alex) was known to be aggressive was when he once accompanied Andreas to the house of a debtor. Other evidence of Andreas's compassionate side surfaced during an early sales trip. Andreas returned from his first sales trip to Russia with no luggage. While the trip was a success, and he took orders for several saws, he also witnessed extreme poverty and consequently gave away all nonessential personal items. It's told he did this numerous times; that's demonstrative compassion.

Andreas Stihl Engineering experienced a period of rapid expansion in product, people, product development, and culture during the 1930s. STIHL patented and introduced several features on the chainsaw—including a swiveling bar, and later a swiveling carburetor, so the saw could be used to fell and buck, and eventually automatic chain oiling.

First STIHL Choir

Perhaps at the urging of his wife, who'd given birth to a son, Hans Peter, Andreas's company produced and sold washing machines for the home. It was during the washing-machine days that Andreas realized the value of keeping mothers happy with an unprecedented two-year warranty. Even though the washing machine line was a success, production and sales lasted only a couple of years. Export sales to other European countries was exhausting the more profitable chainsaw production capacity, so Andreas decided to stop producing washing machines and focus on chainsaws—but not before the birth of his first daughter, Eva. Mrs. Stihl no doubt appreciated the convenience of a washing machine—particularly years later, during the lean war years, when, often alone, she tended to four children and hundreds of chickens.

The festive STIHL culture began to take shape when a group of STIHL employees gathered voluntarily after work to sing. Perhaps their mood was elevated by Germany's most popular drink: beer. The STIHL choir was officially founded in 1935, and eventually

recorded several albums. The STIHL choir continues to this day—
thus the celebratory culture of STIHL is maintained. (See http://
www.STIHL.com/STIHL-choir.aspx.)

Andreas always believed that the best advertising was word
of mouth: users telling other users. Since STIHL had become an
international company, Andreas was able to be convinced of the
value of an advertising agency. STIHL contracted with its first
advertising agency in 1936 and developed a new logo. Keeping
with Andreas's philosophy, STIHL's early advertising and product
literature included customer testimonials, a precursor to today's
"Real People STIHL People" campaign.

The first STIHL saws exported to North America arrived in
1932, but not until the fall of 1936 did Andreas Stihl make his legendary sales trip across Canada. After arriving by ship, perhaps
in Nova Scotia, he had no trouble selling all fifteen of his demonstration models to nearby sawmills, which he would soon realize
was a mistake. Having in hand only drawings of his revolutionary product, he then traveled four thousand miles to the west coast
of Canada, the region known worldwide for its mammoth trees.
Based on the schematics, Bloedel, Stewart, and Welch, of Vancouver,
British Columbia—Andreas's primary target for the transatlantic
trip—were keenly interested in becoming the Canadian importer,

but they insisted on first seeing the actual product in operation. Andreas then backtracked across the entire length of Canada, purchased several of the saws he'd sold only weeks earlier, returned to Vancouver with the repurchased demos, and sealed the deal.

Andreas Stihl traveled over sixteen thousand miles inside Canada to sell fifteen saws and successfully established STIHL's first importer in the western hemisphere. In so doing, he proved that he was not only a brilliant engineer and inventor, but also a tenacious salesman. Tired, exhausted, and likely homesick after making the longest sales call in STIHL history, the father of the chainsaw boarded the ship for home. Mr. Stihl, the man who founded the company, still holds the record for miles traveled to sell fifteen saws. Soon thereafter, under the name of Mill & Mine Supply, the D. J. Smith Company of Seattle, Washington, was established by Bloedel, Stewart, and Welch as the first STIHL dealer in the United States.

World War II was a worldwide crisis that resulted in countless material losses, shifts in provincial borders, and the loss of nearly 85 million people when including death by war-related disease and famine. Even though Andreas Stihl Manufacturing lost their primary manufacturing facility and—possibly, of more value— their patent protection, Andreas—persistence personified—picked up the pieces and continued on his methodical innovative journey.

During the war, STIHL manufactured thousands of saws for the German government. The manufacture of those saws—once the lifeblood for A. STIHL during wartime and eventually the reason Andreas was temporarily incarcerated by the French— became the bane of A. STIHL. Saws purchased by the German government during the war began to show up and soon temporarily flooded the chainsaw market.

Hans Peter Stihl

Andreas, ever the finder of solutions, first invented and then developed a single-cylinder diesel engine and began manufacturing and selling tractors to generate revenue and keep the company afloat. Andreas learned the critical importance of service after the sale while selling tractors. It was possibly during that time when service became a prime requirement for STIHL sales. The tractor era was successful for more than ten years, but like the washing machine experience, it was discontinued so Andreas could once again focus on handheld—his original and primary passion.

Andreas didn't let the success of the tractor quench his quest to build a lighter and better tree-felling machine. First the BL and then the lighter BLK were introduced in the early 1950s. BLK stands for Benzin, Leich, Kettensag, or Gasoline, Light, Small. The BLK was STIHL's first legitimate one-man gasoline chainsaw and eventually lead to the inspiration for the reintroduction of STIHL in America.

The Mall Tool Company of Chicago, while not an official importer, was established as STIHL's first partner in the United States during the 1930s. STIHL also provided Mall with stamped parts for making saw chains.

That relationship was meaningful but short-lived, lasting until World War II when STIHL lost all patent protection. This provided great benefit for US manufacturers, who quickly copied STIHL's patented designs. In a letter dated April 5, 1948, from Arthur Mall of Mall Tool Company to Andreas Stihl, Mr. Mall writes, "All of the saws made in the United States and Canada and used during World War II were more or less a copy of your design of chainsaw. Most of the chainsaws that are being used today are a copy of your design."

STIHL's standard-setting impact on the logging industry in the United States began during the 1930s and never ceased—albeit by several different names, especially Mall. While the war took its toll on the popularity of products made in countries that had been our enemies, efficiency and demand for quality eventually began to heal war wounds not much more than a decade old. Of course, there's more to the story.

MALL TOOL COMPANY

SOUTH CHICAGO AVENUE
CHICAGO 16, ILLINOIS, U.S.A.
EXPORT DEPARTMENT

CABLE ADDRESS "MALLTOOL" CODES USED: BENTLEY'S COMPLETE A. B. C. 6th EDITION ACME PHRASE

April 5th, 1948

Mr. Andreas Stihl
14 A Stuttgart-Bad Cannstatt
Rosenaustrasse 30
Wurtemberg
Germany
(American Zone)

Spruchkammer
Eingang:

Dear Mr. Stihl:

I read with interest your letter of February 25th, 1948, and wish to say tha
I too sympathize with you at the present time, because I know of the fine
engine design work you have done in showing the entire world how to make
a portable gasoline engine timber saw. All of the saws made in the United
States and Canada and used during the World War II were more or less a copy
of your design of chain saw. Most of the chains that are being used today
are a copy of your design. Of course we have greatly improved your original
design as you demonstrated in Canada and the United States about twenty year
ago. I have always believed in giving credit where credit is due, and your
light weight, 4 horse power saw showed us the way here in the United States
and Canada how to really make a practical chain saw. Our United States
army bought at least 10,000 chain saws which were more or less a copy of
yours. The chain saw you are making now is of good design and shows good
engineering.

One reason for wanting to cooperate and become financially interested with
you was because of your practical design of chain saws. We are now
manufacturing one hundred 7 horse power gasoline engine chain saws per day.
Besides this, we are manufacturing numerous electric and pneumatic chain
saws and bow saws. Our factory here in Chicago consists of 400,000 square
feet of floor space; so that will give you some idea of our activity. We
will be employing 1,400 men and women within thirty days. We now employ
over 1,200 people.

We have numerous portable power tools that you could manufacture and dis-
tribute for the European market, which would greatly help the economic
situation in Germany. In addition to this we could easily inaugurate a
design and research department of German engineers who could work out many
new power driven tools, either pneumatic gasoline engine or electric motor
driven that we could use throughout the world.

I appreciate your situation, and feel certain that if you had not cooperated
with the Hitler Government when it was the only government in Germany, that
you would have suffered great personal injuries. It is unfortunate that the
United States has seen fit to follow a very narrow minded, revengeful,

-2-

April 5th, 1948

Mr. Andreas Stihl

Morgenthau policy that is not in accordance with the majority of the citizen of the United States, and does not meet with their approval. Revengeful, impractical, and uneconimical handling is a very serious problem for the citizens of the United States as well as Europe.

I hope that the United States will soon admit their error and change their policy, which will be more constructive and help us prevent another war.

Yours very truly,

MALL TOOL COMPANY

A. W. MALL

AWM:et

P.S. You can feel free to use this letter where ever you think it will do the most good for everyone concerned.

AWM

Vorstehende Abschrift
beglaubigt:

Rechtsanwalt

Chapter Six

FIRST RISK AND
THEN REWARD

WHILE TURNING THE PAGES OF my mind, it seems I can still recall the odors that accompanied boarding the DC8: burnt jet fuel, mixed with the unique passenger-cabin aromas; a blend of pleasant female fragrances, heavy male colognes, and aircraft upholstery. At the time, the notion of flying to Germany took precedence over what had occurred to make the flight possible and the significance to me of those on the flight.

Once the cabin doors closed, the aroma of dinner wafted from the galley throughout the cabin. The smell of food nudged flight from my primary focus while I made my way down the aisle, making eye contact with countless new faces, hoping dinner would be served soon, and wishing someone would ask me about inertia navigation . . . but not necessarily the Coriolis effect.

To my great joy, the plane had a rear galley just behind Teri's and my row of seats; we'd be among the first to be served. I squeezed past Teri to the window seat, showed her a copy of our flight track, and was dying for her to ask. But navigation never came up; she was too engrossed in a Nancy Drew novel. Once the engines began to spool up, I pressed my face tight against the oval window until I could almost see the entire wing. Dinner service began a few minutes after getting airborne. As exciting as it was, it would be years before I fully realized the significance of the trip.

I'd nearly lost all hope for a return trip to the cockpit when a stewardess with an accent similar to what I'd heard in a James Bond movie told me the captain had asked if I was coming back. "Do know de vey, yes?" she said, smiled, and pointed toward the cockpit. The plane seemed longer than ever while making my way through the maze of people standing in the aisle. The area near the table at the front of the plane was particularly crowded. Gordon, Harding, and Ernie were seated at the table and sharing stories about how long they'd been friends and how they'd come to be selling STIHL. Anxious to get to the cockpit, I didn't linger long enough to hear any details. I realized years later what I wish I'd known then.

It's interesting to look back and see how history unfolded and to recognize how unrelated events that occurred simultaneously eventually share a mutual destiny.

General George Washington, his aide-de-camp, Alexander Hamilton, and France's General Lafayette once enjoyed a short midday break near a small settlement located alongside the great falls of the Passaic River. Years later, the village would be named Paterson, after then-Governor William Paterson. It's thought that the town was thus named in exchange for Governor Paterson granting monopoly status to a river-dependent milling enterprise of Hamilton's: the Society for Establishing Useful Manufactures (SEUM). The society's primary goal was the piracy of British trade and manufacturing techniques—essentially, industrial espionage. SEUM played a significant role in moving the United States away from agrarian dependence and toward its eventual industrial might. Years later Paterson was home to a company that combined industrial genius with the needs of the agrarian sector: STIHL.

At possibly the same time that Andreas Stihl was making his legendary trek across Canada, Gordon and Ernie were playing football at Ridgewood High in Ridgewood, New Jersey; their classmates included Harding Smith. The three of them would be essential members of the team selling STIHL at STIHL American, but that would be nearly twenty years later. Much would occur between their high school days, Andreas's prodigious crisscross of Canada, and establishment of STIHL American.

In the meantime, Andreas's many successful sales trips resulted in dramatic growth for A. STIHL Manufacturing in Stuttgart, Germany. Pictured is Andreas standing proudly with his team of technicians outside the Stuttgart factory. The war initially reduced sales for STIHL, and several workers had to be dismissed, with worse occurring later. Since Stuttgart was a major industrial center, Royal Air Force bombers indiscriminately destroyed factories of any nature. STIHL was not spared and, suffering the same fate as all the others, was completely destroyed. There's a German saying, "a new broom sweeps clean," and in STIHL's case, a new bomb swept clean. Fortuitously, Andreas had already begun moving operations to a village just outside Stuttgart. The destructive bombings accelerated plans for the move to what would become STIHL's permanent world headquarters—an abandoned paper mill in the Rems River valley near Waiblingen.

Following high school, Gordon first attended Wesleyan University and then, at the outset of World War II, transferred to the

Citadel. Larger than most and physically strong, Gordon was assigned a machine gun and lugged it from skirmish to skirmish across France and Germany, losing many close combat friends along the way. Coincidentally, he was recognized as a graduate of Wesleyan College roughly the same day he went ashore in France. Along with the Seventh Army—one hundredth infantry, he fought his way across France and Germany, and by war's end, he ended up just northeast of Stuttgart, near a town to which he'd providentially return in 1958: Waiblingen.

After war's end, Gordon finished his military duty serving in Germany as an English teacher. During that time he became well acquainted with the Seyfert family, of Seyfert corrugated box fame. He was frequently posted to their factory as a guard, and he developed a relationship with the Seyferts that would be beneficial to STIHL in later years.

In 1949—about the same time that Andreas was developing the BL, BLK, a diesel engine, and a tractor—Gordon received an honorable discharge from the army and took a job with Bliss Exterminator. A salesman at heart, and impressed with the sprayer he used while treating building after building in the greater New York area, he decided to pursue a sales position with the manufacturer of the sprayer, Hudson Sprayer of Chicago.

Diesel-Motor Typ 135

Gordon's biggest customer for the sprayer was the Arthur D. Peterson Company, a supplier of golf course equipment, owned by noted golf-course architect, Al Tull. Al was so impressed with Gordon that he offered to set up a wholesale division that Gordon would run. The new division was Estate Equipment Company, and it was there that Gordon found his niche.

While at Estate Equipment, Gordon's passion for chainsaws and saw chain grew. He and Al created Tull-Williams, a company focused on the sales of Canadian saws, Oregon chain, and related items. Gordon learned the chainsaw market and gained an understanding of the value of trust between the manufacturer and seller when Canadien made the abrupt and unscrupulous decision to eliminate the wholesale distributor from the sales channel.

Rather than fold the books and close the doors, Gordon harkened to a recent trip to the Oregon saw-chain manufacturer where he'd observed loggers using saws being tested by Oregon on behalf of STIHL. The spokesman, possibly Virg Hatfield, claimed the saw was made with Swiss perfection. The saws, of course, were STIHL's BLK, and the loggers—perhaps unable to correctly pronounce the name, but knowing their German origin—equated the quality to that of the precision of a Swiss watch. They did not know that the saw's namesake was actually born in Switzerland. The chain on the saws was possibly a copy of STIHL's no-longer-protected saw chain patents. The loggers expressed frustration at not being able to easily acquire additional saws. They also mentioned that with more power, the saws could be direct drive and consequently, lighter. A seed had been planted in fertile ground. The grand plan began to take shape in Gordon's mind's eye.

During the ensuing months, a series of letters were exchanged between Gordon and STIHL's export manager Reinhold Guhl. The letters from Gordon included more than simply an inquiry for product distribution; he had a technical suggestion as well.

Almost ten years to the day since Andreas Stihl had received a letter from Arthur Mall acknowledging the copying of STIHL patents by most saw manufacturers in America, Andreas sent a letter to Gordon inviting him to Germany. Gordon and his high school friend—by then a highly respected businessman—Harding Smith, would be making the trip. Both hoped to soon be partners in a new endeavor. STIHL would soon be returning to America.

1958: the Dodgers left Brooklyn, the United States launched its first satellite, Elvis joined the army, and two Jersey business partners boarded a plane at New York's Idlewild International Airport bound for Germany. Millions were captivated by the first three events; few, other than family, noticed the latter. Gordon Williams and his lifelong friend, Harding Smith, had high hopes, charisma, and a business plan. It would take all they had to offer in order to make the deal with Andreas Stihl, the revered father of the chainsaw.

Harding's great-grandfather—Samuel Smith, an Irish immigrant—worked for both Roger's and Danforth locomotive in Paterson, New Jersey, before forming his own company, Smith Engines. Danforth and Rogers, with Smith-designed engines, manufactured the *Texas* and the *General*. Both locomotives where involved in the Great Locomotive Chase of the Civil War. The participants were awarded the very first Congressional Medals of

Honor by President Lincoln and were featured in a 1956 Disney movie — *The Great Locomotive Chase*.

Gordon was the charismatic marketer of the team. Gordon's great-grandfather, Henry Augustus Williams, was a confidant of President Lincoln, a prominent lawyer in Paterson, New Jersey, and the Civil War mayor of Paterson. Henry's father-in-law sold agriculture equipment. At the same time, on his mother's side, Gordon's great-grandfather, James Johnson, not only owned a hardware store in Paterson but also designed products for Samuel Colt, who had a factory in Paterson. At the time, Paterson, having been established and planned by Alexander Hamilton, was the industrial center of the United States. Gordon's Garden State lineage included politics, law, industry, and agriculture. His roots were deep and diverse, and his character sound.

The extraordinary qualities of both Samuel Smith and Henry Williams had survived multiple generations and were manifested when Gordon and Harding boarded their first flight to Germany to establish an international business agreement. Eventually, as the result of a tiny component of international trade, thousands of lives in the United States would be dramatically enhanced economically and vocationally. The brand, already on its way to becoming number one in the world, would ultimately be manufactured in the United States and become the leading brand worldwide.

Together, Gordon and Harding had more than hope, charisma, and a plan; they had a bond built on values, fidelity, loyalty, and integrity. While not exactly family, their relationship was several generations deep. Their great-grandfathers, grandfathers, and fathers had been close friends — and that bond had been handed down through the generations.

Both men were slowly making their way toward the gate door and waving good-bye to a host of friends and family gathered at the departing gate to see them off on their night flight over the wintry waters of the Atlantic. This was back in the days before strict security measures prohibited those who were not passengers from gathering in the gate area.

As soon as they passed through the gate door and onto the tarmac, a gust snapped the heavy steel door shut behind them, filling both men with a no-turning-back-now sensation. The two hesitated under the protection of a small canvas awning, with its frayed edges dripping and flapping in the wind. A ramp attendant holding an oversized umbrella motioned for them to follow him. Gordon draped his large arm across the thin but formidable shoulders of his friend, Harding, gave him a lingering pat, grinned, and said, "Here we go, Smish." Gordon had nicknames for everyone—Smish likely being a combination of Smith and Irish. With that, the two men, holding their fedoras with one hand and clutching their briefcases with the other, hustled through a chilling, breezy winter drizzle under the partial protection of the attendant's umbrella, to the waiting Pan Am, emblazoned *Super Connie*. They were the last to board.

Later that same year, 1958, President Eisenhower would participate in a ceremony christening Pan Am's first Boeing 707 designed for transatlantic flight. The christening ceremony kicked off an elaborate celebration that included a planeload of dignitaries being flown to Paris for a party hosted by Juan Trippe, founder of Pan Am. While Pan Am's inaugural charter flight would inspire Gordon to do something similar eight years later, the DC8, the inspiration, and much more were yet to come. In 1958 the Lockheed, pressurized Super Connie Electra—crude by today's standards—was the pinnacle of luxury in transatlantic travel.

Albert Gore, Jr, ten years old at the time, was enrolled in DC's prestigious St. Alban's Elementary school and had yet to invent the Internet. Tim Berners-Lee, the true inventor of the World Wide Web, was only three and learning English in England. Suffice it to say, communications at the time were archaic by twenty-first century standards. Gordon and Harding wouldn't be in contact with family until their return. Phone calls via the transatlantic cable—at twelve dollars per three-minute, barely audible increments, combined with the time change—weren't feasible or affordable.

After climbing the air stairs, Gordon and Harding were greeted by a friendly, statuesque stewardess who took their overcoats while another showed them to their linen-draped seats before taking their drink order. They joined a nearly full flight of well-dressed passengers, men in vested suits and ladies in dresses—typical airline travel attire in 1958.

Knowing Harding liked to keep an innocent eye on the ladies, Gordon settled his large frame into the window seat. While Harding enjoyed his nerve-calming Irish whiskey, Gordon sipped on a Scotch, gazed out the oval window, watched the two engines on his side roar to life, and listened while the same occurred on the aft. Each engine start was followed by a fuselage-engulfing plume of smoke caused by oil that had leaked into the combustion chambers of the lower half of the eighteen cylinders on the massive Pratt & Whitney radial engines. Since transatlantic passengers were generally veteran flyers, the spectacular start-up exhaust usually went unnoticed, unlike domestic flights when the sudden belch had to be explained to nervous first-timers.

The unsynchronized, low-frequency wha-wha-wha of the giant supercharged engines was sufficiently loud enough to drown out the annoying alcohol-induced passenger-cabin chatter.

The notion that he'd be making the same flight eight years later, along with 144 of his customers, in a privately chartered KLM DC8 jet, was beyond Gordon's wildest imagination.

Harding noticed that the hem on the stewardess's dress extended below her knees, indicating she was new, possibly in training, and still on probation, which meant they'd receive excellent service. The more tenured stewardesses were allowed to shorten the hem and sometimes depended on their athletic-looking legs to substitute for attentiveness to gentlemen business travelers. While the primary duty of the stewardess was passenger safety, and each was well trained in emergency procedure and first aid, the flying public would soon expect the stewardess to function as an in-flight waitress.

After a final spray of deicing glycol, the Connie taxied into position. The pilot stood on the brakes while the copilot moved the throttles, propeller pitch, and fuel mixture full forward. Once satisfied all four engines were developing full power, the captain released the brakes, allowing the massive propellers to turn horsepower into thrust by taking continuous giant bites of cold, dense air, tossing each bite rearward and moving the plane rapidly down the runway and finally airborne. Passengers sitting abeam the propellers orbit hadn't a clue regarding metal fatigue or the consequence of the tiniest sliver of propeller, damaged by runway debris, breaking away and the chance that centrifugal force would carry the sliver through the cabin. Sometimes it's best not to know.

Gordon looked out the window and enjoyed the flickering night lights of New York City until the plane was completely enveloped in the overcast; he then turned to Harding, "What time is it, Smish?"

"Why don't you wear a watch, Gordy?" Harding had never

known Gordon to wear a watch or anything resembling jewelry. It was a rhetorical question.

"Why should I?" Gordon asked. "You always have one." Harding's laugh was always one of those contagious full-body affairs that were impossible to go unnoticed and, in that instance, unfelt. His entire seat, along with the drop-down tray for the passenger sitting behind him, bounced with each chuckle. "I tell you what," Gordon continued, "If we close this deal, I'll think about asking Ann and the kids to buy me a Cartier for Father's Day."

Harding, caught off guard both by Gordon's willingness to consider wearing a watch, for which countless friends and family would be appreciative, and his knowledge of a very expensive timepiece, was momentarily speechless. Harding finally had the temerity to ask, "Why a Cartier?"

Gordon turned to Harding and gave him a what-planet-are-you-from look and said, "He invented the wristwatch." When Gordon sensed Harding hadn't made the connection, he explained: "Just like Andreas Stihl invented the chainsaw. If I'm going to sell saws made by the man who invented them, then it only makes sense that I wear a watch made by the man who invented them."

"Does that mean you're going to buy a Mercedes too?" Harding asked. Gordon stared out the window and didn't answer right away. By then they'd climbed well above the clouds and were being treated with the light of a full moon's reflection illuminating the undercast like a painter's blank canvas.

"First things first, Smish," Gordon finally murmured.

Harding never gave the time; it didn't matter. As if on cue, both men reached for a cigarette—Harding a Camel no filter and Gordon a Lucky Strike.

Cartier, Gordon explained later, had invented the wristwatch in 1904 for an aviation friend, Alberto Santos-Dumont. Santos-Dumont, a Brazilian, was the first to fly a heavier-than-air craft in France, and he had asked his friend, Cartier, to build him a timepiece that would be easy to access and read while flying when both hands were occupied.

The route from New York to Germany took them northeasterly up the east coast toward Newfoundland and then easterly, skirting the southern tips of ice-covered Greenland, and then over relatively ice-free Iceland—the two islands having been named prior to the shift in the northerly flow of the warm Gulf Stream current. The route then turned southeasterly over Scotland, England, eventually France, and finally toward Stuttgart, Germany.

Typical flight crews at the time were Army Air Corps veterans. While a transatlantic flight wasn't to be taken lightly, crewing a well-maintained Lockheed Constellation over friendly territory, from which nobody would be attempting to shoot them down, and through airspace absent of menacing Luftwaffe Messerschmitts, made the flights seem, relatively speaking, akin to a proverbial walk in the park.

Each crew flying the transpolar route over the Arctic was equipped with a winter survival kit, including a 7.62 mm AR10 carbine for use against polar bears, in the event the plane was forced down onto the polar ice. The passengers—comfortably seated in the warm pressurized cabin, having enjoyed a gourmet dinner, and somewhat sedated, either from alcohol or exhaustion—were oblivious to the perils of crossing the Atlantic at night and unaware of the rarely necessary assortment of arctic survival equipment. Most were excited about the exotic nature of transcontinental air travel, which was still in its infancy; others were hyperventilating into their sick sacks. The Titanic had long since been forgotten.

Gordon finished his Scotch, placed his briefcase on the lowered seat-back tray, and was enveloped with the musky smell of the attaché case's damp top-grain cowhide. After retrieving a file of documents covering the chainsaw market in the United States and the attributes of two-step distribution versus dealer direct, he closed the briefcase and reviewed the documents, committing the information to memory. It was a routine he'd repeat several times during the long flight. The purpose of the trip was to discuss a direct drive chainsaw and gain the exclusive rights for selling STIHL in America. He needed to be prepared for any and all questions pertaining to the market potential and his carefully thought-out sales strategy.

Gordon and Harding, two men of extraordinary character, were about to meet their match and more. They'd need to impress Andreas Stihl, the inventor of the portable gasoline chainsaw, whose brusque German demeanor was legendary.

Flying east through the night, morning comes quickly—literally, eight hours earlier. While it was midnight in New Jersey and the drizzle had turned to snow, the Pan Am flight enjoyed a clear-sky sunrise bathing the Western European continent. The captain's gravelly voice came over the intercom: "Ladies and gentlemen, we're now crossing the border between Germany and France and beginning our descent." Those next to windows looked down and imagined a line across the landscape separating Germany and France. After a short pause, the pilot continued, "We're now crossing the Maginot line," confirming in Gordon's mind that the pilot was an Army Air Corps veteran. Gordon looked around the cabin and knew instantly which passengers had served in Europe during the war: those that had instantly dropped what they'd been reading and were transfixed in time, staring reflectively into space or out a window.

France's line of defense between themselves and Germany had been built in the 1930s and named after their Minister of War, André Maginot. Not visible from the air, the Maginot consisted of twenty-two large underground bunkers and thirty-six smaller fortresses and numerous blockhouses, all fortified with weapons and supplies and connected by rail. It was a feat of major undertaking and, at the time, thought to be a work of genius. However, the fortifications hadn't been placed in the areas of rugged terrain, and the tenacious Germans had simply marched through those areas during the war, deeming the costly building of the French fortresses futile.

Gordon's mind was flooded with things he'd been told and those he'd experienced firsthand near the French-German border. Earlier, he'd studied a map published by Pan Am of the likely route of the flight and had noticed they'd be flying south of—but near—the Argonne, where Alvin York, during World War I, had valiantly led a small squad on a mission, subsequently received a battlefield promotion to sergeant when all the officers in his squad had been killed, and was later awarded the Medal of Honor.

Gordon then tearfully recalled a couple instances of his own World War II experience. In one instance he'd been transferred to a new unit that had lost its machine gunner. Days later he learned that a close friend, the one who replaced him in the former unit, had been killed in combat, and Gordon realized that it could have been he. And another close call was when his unit had taken refuge in a farmhouse. Thinking it a safe distance from the fighting, Gordon found an upstairs bedroom. He'd only slept an hour or so when he awoke and decided it better to return to the main floor and join the rest of his unit. No sooner had he left the bedroom when a rocket hit the house destroying most of the second floor. He would have been killed had he not returned to the main floor just moments prior to the attack. He learned later of his mother's premonition that he'd been in danger on that particular day. And she'd had similar premonitions that eerily aligned with days when Gordon's unit had experienced heavy fighting and casualties. Knowing that Andreas Stihl had supplied the German army with chainsaws, and served a short time in prison for doing so, Gordon then began to worry of lingering animosity that might remain with Mr. Stihl or any others with whom he'd be meeting.

Gordon elbowed Harding awake and let him know they'd begun their descent into Stuttgart. Neither had been able to get much rest on the flight, and Harding was a little miffed that Gordon had awoken him just when he'd finally succeeded in restful sleep. Gordon convinced Harding that he'd been asleep for over an hour when, in fact, he'd only dozed off moments earlier. They discussed the legend, the man recognized as the father of the chainsaw, and the purpose of the trip. It would be the biggest deal of their lives. The task before them was to convince Andreas Stihl and his staff that their vision and their well-laid plan was the right strategy with which to reenter the American market.

It wasn't as if the duo were arriving hat in hand, unannounced, at the doorstep of STIHL's Waiblingen headquarters. After weeks of correspondence with Reinhold Guhl, STIHL's VP of export, explaining the proposition, they were anxious to meet him. Reinhold, waiting for them as soon as they'd cleared customs, welcomed them to Germany and drove them to one of Stuttgart's premier landmarks: the Turm Hotel, a towering historic edifice of German architecture, complete with a Mercedes star mounted on the roof. It is situated adjacent to the main train station and Stuttgart's famous Koenigstrasse (King Street), the longest pedestrian street in Europe.

The meeting only lasted a few hours but had a decades-long impact on many families all across America. Reinhold Guhl, Andreas's VP of marketing worldwide, served as translator. Even though Reinhold spoke excellent English, based on subsequent meetings, Reinhold's translation during that first meeting is anybody's guess. Reinhold liked what he saw in Gordon and Harding and liked what he heard in their plan and made sure the translation to Andreas was favorable. Mr. Stihl, occasionally capricious, trusted Mr. Guhl's judgment; a one-page contract was prepared and executed. It's clear by the terms of the contract that Andreas was more concerned with performance than promises, which reminds me of one of George Washington's favorite sayings: *facta non verba*, deeds not words. Gordon would soon learn whether his notion of the potential for sales of direct drive saws would materialize. It would.

Mr. and Mrs. Reinhold Guhl, Mr. Andreas Stihl, Gordon Williams

During this meeting or soon thereafter, Gordon introduced STIHL to the Seyfert family. STIHL eventually began using Seyfert cardboard boxes. At this writing, STIHL continues to use containers produced by Seyfert's successors.

Due to westerly winds, transatlantic flights heading west (home) are much longer than those heading east, but it didn't seem that way for Gordon and Harding. Regardless of the confidence with which they'd convinced friends and family of the logic of the trip, and the repeated reviews of their presentation before and during the flight, they'd been fraught with fear of failure and doubt, aggravated by a severe case of insomnia. So, even though the flight home was several hours longer—including a fuel stop in Shannon, Ireland, where they'd purchased several bottles of Irish whiskey—it seemed shorter for three reasons. First, they had in hand a one-page contract signed by Andreas Stihl, granting them the exclusive rights for selling STIHL in the United States. And, second, they had a celebratory gift from Andreas, a bottle of kirschwasser, literally translated "cherry water"; it was anything but. Kirschwasser, a brandy or schnapps, is sometimes called "Bavarian kerosene." At eighty proof, it is a long way from a breakfast fruit drink. The third reason was packed in the luggage compartment below: two STIHL BLK saws, similar to what Gordon had seen during the Oregon visit.

The other passengers on the flight were delighted when sleep finally came for the raucous, celebrating American businessmen. Gordon and Harding arrived home having slept for nearly eight hours but not necessarily feeling refreshed. They'd soon need a bigger warehouse and more money.

The two men were about to embark on a business venture fraught with risk that would first drain their financial resources before returning a handsome investment on their time, talent, and treasure.

Waiblingen-Neustadt, March 5, 1958.

Contract

It is hereby agreed that the Williams-Smith Company upon fulfillment of the following terms shall be appointed exclusive importer for the United States of America for a period of 5 years which may be renewed one year prior to the termination of that contract. The Williams-Smith Co. retains the right to assign this contract to another Company.

The Williams-Smith Company agree to purchase saws from Andreas Stihl, Maschinenfabrik, in quantities of not less than 100 per shipment and will pay for same 15 % deposit with order and the balance night-draft B/L.

At the option of the Andreas Stihl, Maschinenfabrik, this contract may be cancelled providing the Williams-Smith Co. do not purchase the following number of saws per year; the year in which the following quotas are to be made shall commence as of the first shipment of direct-drive saws:

First year:	500 saws
Second year:	2000 saws
Third year:	3000 saws
Fourth year:	4000 saws
Fifth year:	4000 saws.

It is further agreed that on submission of tear sheets and paid advertising invoices Andreas Stihl, Maschinenfabrik, will credit 50 % of said invoices up to a maximum of $ 2.- per saw purchased by the Williams-Smith Company.

For the Williams-Smith Company   For Andreas Stihl, Maschinen-
                                                           fabrik

_____   _____
                                                  (Andreas Stihl)

Chapter Seven

STIHL AMERICAN

As soon as possible following the 1958 trip, Gordon and Harding placed full-page ads in *Chain Saw Age*, the premier chainsaw magazine at the time, soliciting STIHL dealers and distributors nationwide. Response to the ad provided a long list of promising leads.

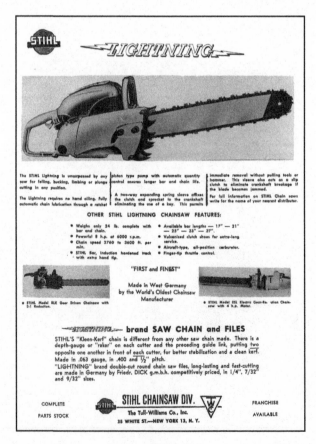

Gordon and Harding's plan called for regional distributors or agents to be established throughout North America. Andreas Stihl's immutable requirement was that the end user be trained regarding the proper use of the saw and that spare parts be readily available to support inevitable breakdowns. Gordon's immutable requirement was that the two-step wholesale distribution strategy be sacrosanct. The two prescient requirements have stood the test of time and are considered STIHL's primary keys to success.

Gordon began an exhaustive travel schedule, first visiting those already familiar with STIHL—known in sales as the proverbial low-hanging fruit. Andy Davidson, owner of United Welding Company of Wellington, Ohio, was the first distributor to be established in America. United Welding served Northern Ohio for several years.

CAMPER outfitted as a show room is used by Mr. and Mrs. Jack Reade in their extensive traveling throughout the East and Middle West in visiting most of their many customers four times a year. Shown with the Reades are their two Great Dane dogs.

Jack Reade's Reade Electric, Walterboro, South Carolina, was the second distributorship to be established. Reade, dealing primarily in Milwaukee electric tools, was unique in that they handled only the electric saws. This was Jack's second trip to STIHL. A 1959 trip to Germany had resulted in him being the first American distributor to visit the STIHL headquarters and his decision to carry the line of electric saws. Jack and his wife, Elizabeth—traveling in a crew cab GMC pickup—established STIHL dealers with the electric saws from Maine to Texas and all states east. Eventually, sales of electric saws were handled by full-line distributors who dealt directly with Reade.

In less than two years, Gordon established more than a dozen additional STIHL distributors across America. Among them was Aldridge Power Company, who hosted the first STIHL Distributor Meeting on September 19, 1959.

First Meeting of STIHL American distributors – September 1959.
Rear (L-R): Walter Aldridge, Harry White, Mr. and Mrs. Jack Reade,
Louis Pfeiffer, W. A. McDonald, John Woody, Luke Aldridge, Charles
and Frank Happ. Front: Zampa Brady, Gordon Williams, Emil Meier,
J. C. Cannon, Reinhold Guhl, Andrreas Stihl, Carl Riddle

Aldridge Power Mower Company of Durham, North Carolina, covered North Carolina and Southern Virginia. Aldridge was founded in 1954 by brothers Luke and Walter Aldridge and John Woody. Luke was the general manager, Walter the service manager, and John took charge of sales. John, having played football at Duke, retained his cement-block physique long after his playing days ended. His powerful build, combined with an effervescent personality and refined swashbuckling aura, gave him a natural room-filling, commanding presence. After enjoying several successful years establishing a network of STIHL dealers throughout the Aldridge territory, John acquired control of the company and renamed it Mid-Atlantic STIHL.

Gordon continued to personally follow up on leads generated by the early magazine ads, establishing a vast STIHL distribution network throughout America. By early 1960 he'd added the following to the growing list of STIHL distributors: Brady Saw Mill Supply, Gassaway, West Virginia; J. C. Cannon, Clinton, South Carolina; Meier and White, Atlanta, Georgia; Ozark Equipment, Rolla, Missouri; Gulf Coast Distributors, Biloxi, Mississippi; Art Gary, Canton, New York; Jack "Chief" Beatty Co., Denver, Colorado; Crader Equipment Co., Marble Hill, Missouri; Ahlborn Equipment Company, Sayner, Wisconsin; Ball Sales and Service, Mount Morris, Michigan; Ralph A. Laubach, Millerstown, Pennsylvania; Farm and Forest, Cincinnati, Ohio; and Whiting Distributing Co., Pulaski, Pennsylvania. By 1965, forty-seven distribution centers, or agents for STIHL, would be established throughout the United States. While each served to establish STIHL in the United States and laid the foundation for future success, only one of the forty-seven originally established—Crader Distributing of Marble Hill, Missouri—survives at the time of this writing.

It's tempting to look back and review the growing list of distributors and recognize the success without realizing the personal, financial, and emotional investment required to overcome repeated countless obstacles and achieve continuing success. All must be taken into account.

Most business failures are due to lack of a good plan, tepid sales, or poor financial management. Some businesses' brush with failure is due to success that exceeds the company's financial capacity to meet all the requirements for rapid growth. It's possible for a business to be profitable but fail due to lack of cash—and so it was with the Tull-Williams company. Gordon and Harding enjoyed more success than they could capitalize. Travel expenses mounted while Gordon continued to establish additional distributors. Gordon and Harding faced additional challenges.

Even though the STIHL saws were more reliable than any other brand available, they weren't trouble free. The first D24s produced experienced considerable problems, some catastrophic. When technical problems arose, in order to establish the brand relatively blemish-free, Tull-Williams stood behind the product beyond the customer's expectations. The expense of doing so mounted. Despite the fact that Harding came from wealth, there was a limit to his personal resources. Unfortunately, during the second year of hard-earned success, expenses finally exhausted cash reserves. Cash, not necessarily sales or profit, is the lifeblood of a business.

Gordon and Harding began 1960 by negotiating an investment by Thermo Dynamics, Incorporated (TDI), a company located in Colorado Springs, Colorado. The details of the agreement aren't available, but it was quickly evident that the new company didn't intend to fulfill its commitments. Gordon and Harding did not appreciate the direction STIHL was headed in the United States with TDI as a partner to Tull-Williams. Gordon and Harding, bearing in mind the foundation they'd laid at great personal sacrifice, spent the better part of 1961 wrestling the exclusive contractual rights away from TDI. With the help of Albert Einstein's personal attorney, by early 1962 the one-page assignable contract was returned to the men with the vision: the Jersey boys.

In an effort to focus their strengths, Gordon and Harding decided to create separate entities. It was then that Gordon created STIHL American and Harding created STIHL Parts. While the companies were financially independent, they were mutually dependent. The new strategy worked beautifully. Both companies experienced rapid sales growth. The same couldn't be said about profits.

At the time, most small-engine manufacturers priced their engines competitively and then shored up profits through parts sales. While STIHL Parts was exceedingly profitable, STIHL American, shouldered with all the expenses necessary to promote and establish the brand, struggled to maintain enough capital to support the exponential growth.

The Stihl family, recognizing the brilliance of Gordon's marketing strategy—evidenced by the rapid sales growth of both companies, and benefiting from the profits on sales to both—agreed to a financial partnership in which STIHL owned 40 percent of STIHL American and Gordon owned 60 percent.

STIHL American and STIHL Parts frugally operated out of Al Tull's warehouse until growth required larger accommodations, at which time both companies moved to a warehouse rented from Joe Minarik—a local cabinetmaker and jack-of-all-trades who'd recently refurbished an abandoned warehouse in East Paterson, New Jersey, not too far from Ridgewood (Gordon and Harding's childhood stomping grounds). The boys never strayed far from their roots physically or ethically.

Chapter Eight

HE HAD A HARVARD MBA, BUT SHE'D FLOWN B-17s

UNMINDFUL OF THE COUNTLESS LONG days, working weekends, and financial risks that had occurred since the signing of the contract to make the chartered flight possible, I squeezed through the crowd gathered at the table and tapped on the cockpit door. The cockpit was crowded—pilot, copilot, and flight engineer. The flight engineer was seated behind the copilot and was watching a set of gauges similar to the ones on the panel in front of the pilot and copilot, including throttle controls. He explained his function—which was to monitor fuel flow, engine condition, and fuel remaining, as well as continually estimate flight, recommend heading changes, and control the cruise power. Since the winds aloft were constantly changing, particularly when we neared the Arctic Circle, frequent course changes were required. There were so many gauges and levers it would have been nearly impossible to know what to look at first or which lever to grab if something when haywire. Of course I wanted to know how fast we were going, so the pilot pointed out the airspeed indicator and then explained how it indicated in knots and also needed to be corrected for altitude and temperature and how the ground speed always differed from true airspeed. I'd read about calibrated airspeed in Dad's pilot ground school book.

Had I realized then what I know now, I'd have been less enamored with the aspects of flight and more in awe of the crew and several passengers, many of whom had served in the Army Air Corps.

I hung around asking questions until the lady that Dad had pointed out as the B-17 pilot asked to speak to the captain. I stared at her in awe, not due to her striking beauty, but mostly because she'd flown a giant airplane. At the time I didn't yet understand the full wartime consequence of the airplane, the inherit risks of flying it, nor the danger she accepted and embraced while doing so. Too many years after I learned Tom and Margo Reck were STIHL distributors from Saint Joe, I learned to respect them for something far greater.

Margo is on the left

He was the son of a Connecticut florist; she was the daughter of a wealthy Missouri banker. He was known for his love of horses; she was known for catching a car on fire with a smoldering cigarette while on the way to grade school. Both were known for their service to the United States. One flew planes and the other went US Navy; they were distinguished members of America's greatest generation.

Tom Reck was born November 1914 in Bridgeport, Connecticut, the home of P. T. Barnum, birthplace of the Frisbee, Subway sandwiches, and once headquarters to numerous well-known companies, including Remington Arms. Situated in the heart of New England, local culture was heavily influenced by British custom, which explains Tom's preference for English riding when, at an early age, he was introduced to horses. Tom never lost the engrained, rigid English demeanor, which served him well while in the military and during his professional career. He eventually developed a dry sense of humor, likely due to his Midwestern wife's influence.

Margot Ford was born October 1917 in Saint Joseph (St. Joe), Missouri—a rugged western frontier town, one of the Oregon Trail's starting points, home to the nation's first expedited mail service, the Pony Express, and located on the famed Missouri River. Even though Margot's family owned Saint Joe's largest bank and were members of local high society, Margot didn't adhere to frumpy social customs and was known for doing the influencing rather than being influenced.

In an effort to quench Margot's precocious spirit and instill in her a sense of refined and proper etiquette, her parents sent her to Smith, a prestigious East Coast girl's school. Instead of seeking a degree in cooking—such as a fellow student at the time, Julia

Child—Margot's gregarious, renegade spirit remained, albeit refined, and she earned a bachelor's degree in architectural design. Margot's time at Smith would be beneficial to her and America.

Tom—fourth from right on front row

One of Margot's housemates while at Smith was Cornelia Reck. Cornelia and other housemates conspired to complete Margot's taming and refinement by fixing her up with Cornelia's older brother, Tom Reck, then attending Dartmouth. Tom was known for being sober, charming, and handsome. Separated by a hundred miles, it was a long-distance relationship with providential promise.

Tom—either to remain in school until Margot graduated or to further his education after Dartmouth—enrolled at Harvard, earning a master's degree in business. After graduation from Harvard, he joined Smith Barney in their New York office.

Margo is on the left

After graduation from Smith, rather than return to Missouri and enjoy a cushy position at the family's bank, Margot accepted an invitation from the Office of Strategic Services—the predecessor to today's Central Intelligence Agency—and moved to Washington, DC, putting her design degree to good use. Margot continued to run, and Tom continued to chase.

A few years went by, and it was June 1941 before Tom and Margo rendezvoused in Saint Joe for an extravagant society event: their wedding. Tom was quoted as saying, "I came for the wedding and never left." However, before year's end, he would be leaving. The country was at war. Tom enlisted, which was typical of most able-bodied men at the time. Margot enlisted too, which was not so typical of women at the time.

Tom was serving aboard the carrier *USS Franklin* when it sustained a crippling kamikaze attack that killed eight hundred sailors in a single blow. Margot, along with twenty-five thousand other women, enlisted in the newly formed Women Air Services Program (WASP) and was among only nine hundred who completed flight training.

Even though the WASP program was technically a noncombat division, several women lost their lives during combat training exercises. Margot flew a variety of planes, including the A-6, P-38, P-40, P-51 fighters, and the famed B-17 bomber—nicknamed Aluminum Overcast by the Germans.

After the war they both got their way: Margot wanted to return to Missouri, and Tom wanted his own business. They settled in Saint Joe after purchasing a growing concern—Ross-Frazer Ironworks—and immersed themselves in the community, albeit in different roles. Tom's childhood passion for horses followed him to Missouri. Soon after getting the business squared away, he made regular trips to the Mission Valley Hunt Club, a two-hour drive from Saint Joe.

Margot's interests were art and athletics. When she wasn't playing golf or tennis or swimming across the Missouri River or dragging one of her daughters along on a paddling excursion, Margot was working on a painting and developing her gifted talent in the arts. Tom and Margot were both active in the community and perpetually involved in philanthropic endeavors.

Ross-Frazer Ironworks eventually became Ross-Frazer Supply, a wholesale distributor covering the northwest region of Missouri, the southernmost counties of Nebraska, and the northernmost counties of Kansas, stretching all the way to the Colorado border. Ross-Frazer sold and serviced a broad line of products and several thousand parts and accessories associated with outdoor power tools, large and small.

STIHL began as a small addition to an already full line of products but grew to be a top-of-the-line product category. STIHL continued to expand the chainsaw line and subsequently entered the lawn and garden category with line trimmers.

Tom was a customer service pioneer, equipping each of his outside salesmen with a two-way radio (before cell phone days) used to call in orders—which in many cases were shipped the same day they were received. Tom's STIHL dealers regularly received their STIHL parts the morning after placing the order, enabling them to provide unparalleled customer service and thereby helping establish the STIHL brand in northwest Missouri and parts of Nebraska and Kansas.

Tom and daughters, Christine and Cricket

Rainer Gloeckle, the STIHL American whiz kid, called on Tom at Ross-Frazier Supply during the early days. He recalls Tom and Margot as being extraordinarily kind, generous, and hospitable. He was invited into their home countless times. During one visit, after becoming ill, both Tom and Margot cared for him for several days until he fully recovered. At the time, he was a young German, far from home, in a foreign country and sick. Rainer will remember the care he received from Tom and Margot forever.

Tom and Margot were unique in many ways. Tom, with a Harvard MBA, could have had a career on Wall Street but chose to settle in the Midwest, raise horses, and sell chainsaws. Margot, a strikingly beautiful and intelligent lady, could have sought a cooking or MRS degree at Smith, but she chose to serve her country. Rather than seeking a glamorous life likely offered her or a desk job at the CIA, she chose to fly America's premier bomber, raise a family, and make a difference in the lives of family, friends, and the local community. Both were devoted patriots, wartime veterans, and exceedingly philanthropic with their time, treasure, and talent. They were America's greatest generation. With people such as Tom and Margot helping establish STIHL, it's no wonder STIHL is today's premier brand of outdoor power tools.

Margot slipped past me and disappeared into the cockpit. At the time I only saw a beautiful lady who'd flown a giant airplane. It wasn't until years later that I'd learn of her extraordinary life and the role she and Tom played in keeping the United States and the world safe.

While researching Tom and Margot's history, it was discovered that their grandson, Christopher, was studying engineering at the University of Stuttgart. A few calls were made and Christopher was accepted for an internship at STIHL's research laboratory in Waiblingen.

Chapter Nine

UNIQUENESS IS COMMONPLACE

ON MY FOURTH PASS BY the galley table, a different set of people had gathered to visit with Gordon. Harding and Ernie had returned to their nearby assigned seats. In their place were Virg Hatfield, Jack Reade, Fred Oswald, and John Woody. Fred was wearing a National Guard uniform—an odd choice of apparel for a visit to Germany, I remember thinking at the time. Fred had come to STIHL American after gaining valuable experience while working at a Madison Avenue advertising agency where he'd been the account executive responsible for the US Army and Ford Motor Company. He was a big fan of *Life Magazine* and began pushing for STIHL to be the first chainsaw company to advertise in *Life*. Fred would also be instrumental in arranging for legendary Green Bay Packer's Ray Nitschke to pose for a poster while holding a STIHL 041AV.

It was visionary men such as Gordon Williams who inspired Norman Vincent Peale to pen "The Power of Positive Thinking." Gordon, the positive thinker and quintessential relationship builder, had immediately reached out to those with whom he was familiar from his days at Estate Equipment and were certain to be interested in handling a fine line of precision-crafted chainsaws— STIHLs. He'd proudly informed them of being officially appointed STIHL's agent for America.

Once Gordon had exhausted leads received as a result of advertising, he drove from state to state and town to town, making unsolicited sales calls—the most difficult kind. As soon as he passed the city limits sign, he'd find a phone booth and search the Yellow Pages for the chainsaw dealer with the largest Yellow Pages ad. Yellow Pages soon became a STIHL dealer requirement and remained so for several decades.

Chapter Ten

STIHL'S FIRST FLYING DISTRIBUTOR

ONE OF GORDON'S EARLY TRIPS included a cross-continent flight returning to Hood River, Oregon, and a sales call on a former logger and, by then, small-engine shop owner: Virgil (Virg) Hatfield. Virg knew the major players in the Northwest logging industry and was already a longtime user of STIHL chainsaws. Virg had been able to acquire BLKs during the 1950s, probably through the Oregon Saw Chain Company's test program. Gordon appointed Virg as both a distributor for the Northwest and an agent for STIHL. As a distributor, Virg began establishing STIHL dealers, mostly logging companies with the capacity to purchase large volumes of saws. As a STIHL agent, Virg assisted Gordon in establishing distributors throughout Washington, Oregon, Montana, South and North Dakota, Wyoming, Idaho, and Alaska. Virg used a Piper Cub to travel throughout his vast territory, making him the first of many flying STIHL distributors.

It's conceivable that Gordon Williams met the chainsaw legend of Hood River while visiting the Oregon chain plant during his days at Estate Equipment. If the two hadn't met, Gordon most likely knew of the reputation of the owner of H&D Logger Supply, Virg Hatfield. Virg's parents had migrated to Oregon from West Virginia. It's possible they were trying to get as far from family

as they could since, during the time of the migration, the Hatfields and the McCoys were bent on killing each other. Some say
the feud was over a disputed pig; others claim the feud was a
remnant of the Civil War. Both families had sided with the Con-
federacy with the exception of one member of the McCoy family,
who'd fought for the Union. No matter, lots of them died during
the nearly thirty-year feud. The Hatfields were the more affluent
of the two families and, fortunately for Virg and his descendants,
were able to escape the carnage.

Virg with his Piper Super Cub

Gordon and Virg maintained a professional respect for each
other, but as the story goes, Virg never cared much for Gordon
or anyone at Tull-Williams, STIHL American, or STIHL Parts. It's
conceivable that Virg—naturally given to holding a grudge, like
so many Hatfields—knew of Harding Smith's relationship to the

locomotives in the Civil War's great locomotive chase, a valiant move on the part of brave Union volunteers and soldiers for whom many were awarded the first Medal of Honor, albeit post-humously, by President Lincoln. Even though the Great Chase raiders were heralded as heroes by the North, they—and anyone connected to them—were considered traitors by Southerners and postwar Southern sympathizers.

While Virg's disdain for the Eastern elite likely stemmed from Southern sympathetic notions, dealing with them posed a con-cession of sorts. But the Mason-Dixon divide likely wasn't the only compromise mulling around in his mind. The Great War with Germany had ended little more than a decade earlier, and STIHLs were made in Germany. Compromises are easier when the gain of doing so is advantageous and when it's clear that others are facing a similar dilemma. Once Virg learned that both Gordon and Harding, the principals of Tull-Williams, had fought for the United States in Germany during World War II (Gordon a machine gunner and Harding a bombardier), he realized he was in good company by promoting the world's finest tree-fell-ing machine, albeit from Germany. Wounds heal quickly when it's to one's advantage that healing occurs. STIHL was anxious to sell saws worldwide, and a lightweight, powerful, dependable saw appealed to America's premier loggers, who didn't care about the saws' country of origin.

Virg was well-known and highly respected throughout the Northwest big-timber region, and for good reason. While serving in the US Navy, he'd spent most of his leisure time boxing, the reminder of which was a crooked nose, leaving him with a vexed and menacing look. Following the navy, Virg worked with a logging crew outside Roseburg, Oregon, the timber capital of the nation, situated in southern Oregon in the Umpqua River valley. He harvested trees—using both chainsaws and the labor-intensive crosscuts—until an injury ended his career as a full-time logger. At that time he purchased a service station in Hood River, some 250 miles away. It's possible Virg, no longer able to log, wanted to get away from logging altogether. The filling station routine didn't suit Virg, and in 1952 when a saw shop came up for sale, he sold the filling station, purchased the saw shop, named it H&D Loggers Supply, and began selling saws, which to him was the next best thing to logging.

After a few years of experience in the saw business and selling a variety of brands, including McCulloch and Remington, he responded to a Tull-Williams advertisement about selling STIHL. Virg was already familiar with STIHL saws, possibly more so than Gordon or Harding. Although rare, older models of STIHLs had trickled into the Northwest; the parts availability was virtually nil. Since Virg was a veteran saw man, he was possibly aware that many features used in American-made saws had been copied from STIHL.

Knowing Virg's reputation and potential, Gordon sent him a saw to demo. After trips to logging camps, felling trees himself — demonstrating both the Super Lightning and his prowess as a logger — and then getting the demo into the hands of respected loggers, Virg had proven both himself and the saw to the most hard-headed and stubborn: America's Northwest woodsmen. Virg knew then he wanted to play a major role in getting STIHL reintroduced in America's Northwest. Virg exemplified the phrase, "If you're going to be a bear, be a grizzly."

Even though Hood River, Oregon, is thousands of miles from Eastern Kentucky, the mentality of the people and geographical terrain is similar. Maybe that's why Virg's parents chose the Northwest; it was like home without the bodacious relatives. Virg's natural independent tendency was to find a solution to a problem rather than complain. He was known to grumble, but the grumbling was generally a conversation he was having with himself during the problem-solving process. Virg's foreboding appearance inhibited anyone from questioning the growling murmurs.

It's not unusual for people from the East Coast, particularly the northeastern area, to think of all states being geographically similar to those of New England: relatively small and condensed. It's possible that with that frame of mind, Gordon agreed that Virg's distribution coverage area would include Washington, Oregon, California, Idaho, Montana, and the Dakotas. While distributors in the East made use of the most efficient and sensible method of transportation in their area — cars, vans, and pickups — Virg chose the most efficient and sensible mode of transportation in which to travel the mountainous and river-strewn Northwest: an airplane.

One of Virg's STIHL customers was also a crop duster with an airplane for sale. When Virg learned of this, the solution to a problem he'd been mumbling about came into view. Virg agreed to purchase the plane, a Piper Super Cub, so long as the crop duster taught him how to fly it. A few flying lessons later and Virg was the owner of an airplane and possessor of a student permit— which technically allowed him to fly legally, without passengers. Technicalities were never an obstacle to a genuine Hatfield.

Virg used the plane to make trips in the rugged Northwest that literally took minutes by air but would require hours by road. Selling chainsaws in the Northwest was different than most other parts of the country. Rather than saw users going into dealers to purchase a saw; those wishing to sell saws had to go to the customer: the giant logging companies. Since most of the logging camps had their own landing strips or gravel roads that served the same purpose, Virg would strap saws into the passenger seat of the two-seat Piper Cub and fly into the camps. Selling saws to a logging concern was a long and arduous ordeal, requiring agreement on the part of the sawyer using the saw, the camp superintendent, and company management. Converting users of the well-known and respected brands such as Homelite, McCulloch, and Remington was slow. The rugged Hatfield problem-solving mentality persisted.

Along with the increased number of STIHL Super Lightnings in the woods came increased numbers of STIHLs getting crushed by trees that didn't fall as intended. Logging camp mechanics at Weyerhaeuser, Georgia Pacific, and other camps had begun cannibalizing crushed units, including the mixing and matching of crankcase housing halves. An unintended consequence was the conversion of finely balanced and relatively vibration-free STIHLs to violently vibrating units that nearly caused cases of nerve damage known as white finger and did cause widespread dissatisfaction among the fearsome loggers.

After a few flying trips to the camps with the highest number of units exhibiting the severe vibration, Rainer Gloeckle, the German whiz kid, quickly diagnosed the problem, but that solution only created another problem. Logging camp mechanics had routinely mixed and matched housings on American-made saws with no noticeable increase in vibration. With Virg's endorsement, Rainer was able to convince the camp mechanics, one at a time, that the Super Lightnings were able to operate with significantly less vibration than American-made saws only because of the German precision, which required matched crankcase housings.

After visiting the area, Gordon likely reached the conclusion that the area was simply too vast for one company and one man; Virg didn't necessarily agree, but then, Virg wasn't the agreeable type. The two eventually settled upon a solution—the appointment of additional distributors throughout the area: Towner, North Dakota; Weippe, Idaho; Phillipsburg, Montana; Portland, Oregon; and Juneau, Alaska, with Virg representing STIHL American to these distributors. Gordon and Harding agreed to place an inventory of parts and saws at Virg's Hood River location for shipment directly to the Northwest distributors. Eventually, Virg moved the joint venture to Chehalis, Washington, a location better suited to serve the vast Northwest, hired a salesman who was also well respected in the logging industry, and renamed the operation Interstate Distributing.

In spite of the additional territory, responsibility, and manpower, Virg continued to personally make the complex sales calls—taking prospective customers hunting, flying to and landing on small islands to hunt for clams, and cramming the Piper Cub with parts and saws and flying them into remote logging camps. Virg tried everything he could think of in an effort to get the loggers who were working for the biggest companies to use STIHL, including assigning Rainer to them. Finally, Weyerhaeuser agreed to take seven new Super Lightnings if the renowned whiz kid would devote a month of his time to tend to the saws and keep them running. Realizing the importance of supporting Virg's success at getting a foot in the door, Rainer agreed to spend a month at the logging camps. The one-month commitment turned into three months, and Weyerhaeuser became STIHL's largest customer in North America. They purchased nearly three thousand saws within the next few years.

Virg delivered the saws to Weyerhaeuser and then shuttled Rainer from camp to camp. It was during one of these trips that the Piper Cub's engine burped, spluttered, and stopped. Silence and sweat overcame both occupants in the cramped plane while Virg searched for and found a place to land. Without an engine, the landing options are strictly limited—particularly in the rugged Northwest; a potato field was the best option. It's said that a good landing is one in which everyone can walk away, and a perfect landing is one after which the plane can be used again. Virg's landing was good but not quite perfect. Since a forced landing was sure to arouse curiosity, and possibly the local authorities, Virg asked Rainer to make himself scarce until a ride arrived. It was then that Rainer learned that Virg didn't have a pilot's license, making it illegal to carry passengers and possibly a crime to crash with one. It was also the day that Rainer decided to begin taking flying lessons, possibly for self-preservation, since he was likely to be spending a great deal of time with Virg.

The narrow escape didn't diminish the relationship between Rainer and Virg, the persistent pilot—even if not technically a licensed pilot—who was the first flying STIHL distributor. Rainer learned to appreciate and admire Virg's tenacious selling approach and his uncanny ability to improvise and visualize solutions.

The advent of more powerful saws by STIHL and other saw manufacturers created unforeseen technical problems, particularly in guide-bar wear. Premium guide-bar manufacturers had begun using Stellite for guide-bar noses. Stellite alloy is a range of cobalt-chromium alloys and carbon designed for wear resistance and is very difficult to integrate onto a bar and is supposedly impossible to repair—except Virg found a way. Virg, not dissuaded by the complex composition of the bar-nose material, developed a technique whereby he could quickly repair the Stellite material on the nose of the long and expensive guide bars. This complex technique, possibly known only to him and no other chainsaw repair shop, saved the loggers a significant amount of time and money. Rather than wait for a new guide bar and being out the expense, Virg would repair the old one quickly and for a fraction of the cost of a new bar. This greatly endeared Virg to the loggers and helped expedite their acceptance of STIHL. Virg shared the technique with his best STIHL dealers, but few were able to master the art of Stellite tip repair.

In another instance he and Rainer collaborated to suggest a gearbox so that the lightweight but powerful saws could handle the long bars necessary to cut the giant trees of the Northwest. The design change was implemented by STIHL on multiple models, but it was short-lived as more powerful saws with no need for a gearbox were soon developed and introduced into the market.

Virg's unceasing desire to improve the STIHL and his constant communication with STIHL Germany through Rainer endeared him to the loggers. It was equally important that he had the respect of STIHL's engineers, particularly the chief engineer and inventor of the chainsaw — Andreas Stihl. Virg was one of the very few distributors to have had the honor of hosting Andreas and Hannelore at his home. Andreas, having had an eye on the big timber country since his legendary trip nearly thirty years earlier, must have been very pleased to visit Virg and see his saws in the hands of hundreds of world-renowned sawyers and being used to harvest the world's largest trees.

Preferring to call on logging camps and large companies, Virg was reluctant to develop a widespread retail dealer base. While Gordon appreciated Virg's success in getting STIHL into the hands of the professionals, he continually challenged Virg to develop dealers who would appeal to the casual user.

Virg's bitter disposition and low opinion of East Coasters would eventually result in a diminishing relationship with STIHL American.

I watched Virg make his way down the aisle and take a seat. Dad had wanted to learn to fly for a long time; Virg was likely the one who helped him make a business case for flying and airplane ownership. Following the trip to Germany, Dad began taking flying lessons. His instructor, a recent high school graduate, was giving lessons while trying to qualify for the army's rigid helicopter flight program. Dad earned his license just before the instructor qualified for the army, became a helicopter pilot, and made the ultimate sacrifice while serving in Vietnam.

Chapter Eleven

THE GARDENER

SOMEWHERE IN FLIGHT, POSSIBLY BETWEEN the isles Greenland and Iceland, the DC8's center aisle was packed with people standing around visiting. A man with smile wrinkles carved into a rugged complexion slowly made his way through the crowd and stopped to say hello to Dad; it was Joe Minarik. Right away I could sense that what Joe lacked in showmanship he made up for in substance. Even at a young age, I could tell the difference. He and Dad talked for more than an hour. Joe's story is inspiring.

Joe wasn't your everyday Joe. His story is important for two reasons: Joe was an essential member of the foundational team of STIHL American, and Joe's journey—typical of those times (people who worked hard, adapted, and made their own success)—would be considered extraordinary today. While Joe's story is amazing, it's not necessarily unique. Most Americans are descendants of people who immigrated to the United States from another country. The United States is a filtered melting pot of people looking to build a better life for themselves and their families as assimilated Americans.

Joseph John Minarik, Joe's father, was born in 1896 in the small village of Zilina, in the state of Trencin, Slovakia. Joseph's family operated a small flour mill and had done so for several generations. In Slovakia, Minarik translates to Miller. It's not clear which came first, the name or the vocation.

Once Joseph reached the age of eighteen, he boarded a steamship for the weeklong voyage to Ellis Island, America. A couple of his friends had already done so, settled in Garfield, New Jersey, and invited Joseph to join them. Once reaching Ellis Island, Joseph had to pass a rigorous health screening. Coming from southern Europe, he also had to pass a political screening—the result of laws put in place following the assassination of President McKinley by an American person of Slavic heritage. After close scrutiny, Joseph was allowed entry to the United States as Joseph Minarik.

Joseph joined his friends in Garfield and, not straying far from his roots, began working in mills, beginning with a nearby woolen mill. Joseph followed opportunity and work, moving to Pennsylvania to work the steel mills, then to Massachusetts's woolen mills, and finally back to Garfield where he met Barbara Pisarcik.

Barbara Pisarcik was born in 1905 in the small village of Frankova, in the state of Spisska, Slovakia. Following the devastation of World War I and losing both parents at a young age, Barbara boarded a ship to Ellis Island, America. She joined older siblings who'd already immigrated and settled in Garfield. Barbara followed a similar path as that of Joseph: first settling in Garfield, then moving to Pennsylvania for work, and then back to Garfield.

By 1925 Joseph found a vocation that promised steady work and one for which there would always be a need: digging graves. He and Barbara, sharing a native tongue and heritage, found the truly significant things they shared in common. Joseph and Barbara were united in marriage in 1925 and had three daughters and finally a son, born 1931, whom they named Joseph. In 1932, in the midst of the Great Depression, Joseph and Barbara—on a gravedigger's income—built a small but sufficient New England house in East Paterson, New Jersey, and made it a home.

Lodi High School served several local communities, many of them populated by Americans having emigrated from southern Europe. While attending Lodi, Evelyn Giba caught Joe's eye. He learned later that her parents had traveled a similar journey as his. It took some convincing, Joe bragged, but he finally convinced Evelyn that they too had the important things in common, and they became a couple. One of the significant things they shared was never having met any of their grandparents, typical of immigrants at the time. This dynamic resulted in close and tight families and ethnic-centric neighborhoods.

Joe's natural sense of responsibility came early. When he wasn't courting Evelyn, he paid close attention to his high school industrial arts teacher and quickly developed a superior skill at woodworking. His instructor, recognizing Joe's passion and advanced skill level, eventually used Joe as an assistant instructor.

It took Joe a few years to muster the courage to pop the question, but sometime during the fall of 1951, he proposed. Days after their engagement, he was served his draft notice—the country being in the midst of the Korean War. Joe and Evelyn, short on time, were united in marriage in early 1952 in a small informal ceremony with the mayor of East Paterson presiding.

Possibly due to his bilingual skills and southern European heritage, Joe was shipped to Germany rather than Korea. And as luck would have it, Evelyn was able to join him during his station in Germany. After completing his military obligation, Joe and Evelyn returned to East Paterson and lived with her parents until they could afford their own place. Their first child, a son, was born in 1957. He too was named Joseph. Four years later they were blessed with another son, Robert, and four years later a daughter, Lynn.

The skills Joe acquired in high school served him well. Following his honorable discharge from the army, Joe found work first at a lumber mill shaping door and window moldings, and eventually building cabinets. After a few years of frugal living, Joe and Evelyn had saved enough money to acquire a shop Joe could call his own. Joe's quality craftsmanship was in high demand, and the business grew; he needed more space. Joe was able to acquire a 3,200-square-foot abandoned warehouse, giving him plenty of space to build all kinds of cabinets and furniture for a variety of clients. The building was more than he needed.

By 1962 another East Paterson, New Jersey, business had grown to the point of needing its own space. Due to a local slowdown in the economy, the cabinet business began to feel the effects. Joe, having space available for rent and having been impressed with Gordon Williams, took advantage of the opportunity; he and Gordon struck a mutually beneficial arrangement.

Following the recent creation of STIHL American, Victor Roessler was sent from Germany to manage receiving, shipping, technical training, and function as a liaison between STIHL American and STIHL Germany. Joe and Victor became close friends.

Victor quickly realized that Joe was more than a landlord and hired Joe to build cabinets specific to STIHL American needs. Joe, seeing that Victor was unable to do his job singlehandedly, spent extra time at STIHL American, on a volunteer basis, helping Victor with warehouse duties. Gordon and Harding, realizing that Victor needed more help to ship units for Gordon and parts for Harding, offered Joe a job. The one-hundred-dollar-per-week offer was less money than Joe was making in his cabinet shop, but Joe says he sensed that he was getting on board with something that would eventually be worth the sacrifice. This prescient sentiment would be sensed and echoed by many others before the end of the decade.

Response to full-page ads running every month in *Chain Saw Age*—starting in 1959 by Tull-Williams and subsequently resumed by STIHL American—continued to pay rich dividends. The single warehouse phone virtually rang off the wall with calls from established STIHL distributors placing orders and those wishing to become STIHL distributors. Joe Minarik— affectionately nicknamed Mockey Mouse by Gordon, and usually shortened to "Mock"—was by then working full-time for STIHL American and took the initiative to have a second phone line installed. Gordon, then being held accountable to a tight budget with the Stihl family—a 40 percent partner—fired Joe for what he thought was an extravagant, unauthorized expense.

The following day a container of saws arrived from Germany. Gordon, shorthanded without Mock, had to help unload the saws. Mock, knowing when the container was scheduled to arrive, came to the warehouse and feigned working on a custom cabinet project. (Recall that Mock owned the warehouse, and it also housed his cabinetmaking shop.) Mock was amused watching Gordon, dressed in formal business attire— tailored suit, tie, and leather-soled shoes—carrying one saw at a time from the container in between answering the phone, which was located at the other end of the warehouse from the dock door. Given time, cooler heads prevailed. Gordon realized the logic in Mock's decision to have a phone line installed adjacent to the dock door, and with most of the saws still needing to be unloaded, he motioned Mock over. The two had a good laugh, and Mock was once again employed by STIHL American.

Bushes Lane Location

Shipping and receiving in those days was not as homogeneous as today; UPS didn't reach nearly all points of the United States as is the case today, and it didn't reach some areas not at all. Parcel post was expensive, slow, and unreliable. Joe improvised when necessary and frequently made trips to the bus station to put critically needed items on a Greyhound bus bound for customers such as Osage Indian Chief Jack Beatty in Denver, Colorado, or remote places further west, such as Hood River, Oregon. Joe took the initiative to do what was reasonably necessary to get the job done.

So, trusted by the Williams family, Joe was frequently asked to make home repairs. On one occasion, the repair of an upstairs window required him to climb onto the roof. Gordon's young daughter Liz thought it humorous to close and lock the window Joe had climbed through. Liz, then unable to get the window unlocked, left to play with friends down the street. Joe was sitting on the roof when Gordon came home for lunch.

Proof that Joe didn't harbor a grudge came years later when Liz, by then driving, came crying to Joe with a problem. She'd used Gordon's car, a beautiful Cadillac, to run an errand. How it happened was never ascertained, but the Cadillac's rear bumper was crushed. Joe suspects Liz backed into a pole. "Can you fix it, Joe?" she asked. Joe's solution was simple and possibly typical of how things work in New Jersey.

"Tell you what," Joe said, and then instructed a teary-eyed Liz to simply back the car into the parking spot with the bumper against the wall. "Your dad is always backing into stuff," Joe assured Liz. "He won't notice for a couple of days, and when he does he'll think he did it." And that's how Joe helped Liz out of that jam.

Gordon frequently assigned a nickname to friends and family, and Joe's son—Joey or Joe Jr.—had one too. Joey relates a time when Joe decided he wanted to try his hand at selling.

Joe Jr. here—or Mockey Mouse Jr. as Gordon would call me. When Gordon asked my dad if he could sell saws, he needed to hit the pavement. So, on Saturdays he would take me to dealerships. They were Homelite and McCulloch dealers. They would throw my father out of the store. "Get that damn German saw out of here." You see, the war was still in people's mind at that time. This is about 1963, 1964. We would leave, and I would say to Dad, "That wasn't very nice of them."

Dad would say, "That's ok."

"Well what are you going to do now?"

He said, "I have Plan B."

He would go directly to tree companies, have them try them out. When they were interested, my father sold directly to them. Then he would set a few of them up as dealers. One of the first was Garden State Tree Service in Old Tappan, New Jersey. Dick Wolfe was the owner. Well, by this time the many dealers that threw my father out of their stores months ago now were interested in becoming a dealer.

My father said, "Hey, you threw me out of your store months ago."

"Yes, but we are sorry for that."

However, he still would sell to tree companies because at the warehouse he had parts and a shop to service the tree guys. He developed a great relationship with the first tree companies like Arrow Tree Service in Old Tappan, New Jersey, and Beucler Tree Service in Tenafly, New Jersey. He would set up dealers that would have shops set up in their basements of their house or in their garages.

He would say to me, "Joe, this is where it all starts. Eventually, they will be able to open up a store."

Among the first was Dan Dunn of Haverhill, Massachusetts, and Bob Fremgen of Midland Park, New Jersey. And so, the STIHL train was picking up speed. I have to say, every customer liked my father, and later when I went into the business, customers liked me. Not only were they customers but friends.

Mock would be temporarily fired once more for purchasing a fork truck without permission. By then, containers coming in and orders being shipped out had reached a volume that fully justified a fork truck. Once Gordon realized the gain in efficiencies provided by the fork truck, Mock was reinstated.

In a recent, seemingly never-ending phone conversation with Dan Dunn—an Army Sargent E-5 who served in Korea during the Vietnam era and one who doesn't mince words—Dan said the following repeatedly: "Joe could do anything; the guy was amazing. I'd do anything for Joe or Joey." I got the impression that "anything" wasn't hyperbole. During Joe's dying days, Dan rarely left Joe's bedside.

Joe's capabilities didn't end with cabinetmaking or warehouse management or selling STIHL. Soon after being introduced, the 040, like the 07 before it, suffered vapor locking when used in warmer climates. Joe developed an asbestos gasket that resolved the issue. His fix was adopted by the engineers in Germany. John Williams recalls all family members being tasked with cutting out pieces of asbestos gaskets to get a quick fix into the field.

Joe was never given credit for the first handheld blower prototype he once cobbled together using a fan mechanism and a STIHL model 08 chainsaw. Sometime after STIHL American ceased to exist and had been taken over by STIHL Inc. of Virginia Beach, Joe gave his prototype to a STIHL marketing executive. The blower wasn't seen for a couple of decades, and when it was eventually discovered in a California warehouse, by then it had been further modified. The blower now hangs in STIHL's Virginia Beach museum.

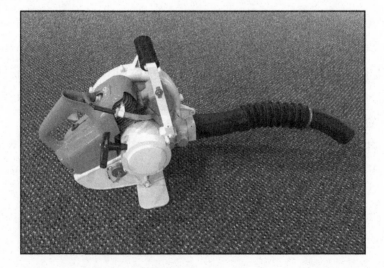

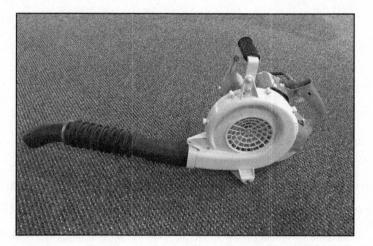

Of all the God-given talents Joe possessed, he most treasured his garden. Asked how he'd like to be remembered, Joe preferred to be thought of as a gardener. His yard was a testament to his wish.

Chapter Twelve

THE WHIZ KID

WITH NEW DISTRIBUTORS BEING ESTABLISHED monthly and distributors establishing new dealers daily, sales exceeded all expectations; the whiz kid had his hands full. Everyone in the logging industry was clamoring for a STIHL—or so it seemed to those working the warehouse at STIHL American. The addition of a phone line and acquisition of a fork truck helped increase warehouse efficiencies, but another issue was brewing that would require help from Germany—technical failures. While the STIHL quickly gained a reputation for being light, powerful, and the most dependable saw in the woods, the STIHL wasn't trouble free—few engines that run at high RPM in dusty conditions are. Help was on the way from Germany via Sweden.

Users of other brands had grown to expect mechanical failure and generally replaced a failing unit with a new one. A typical dealer's back lot included a growing mound of discarded saws, theoretically to be used as spare parts. The problem with this logic was that the part that failed most frequently was the same on all units, so the mounting chainsaw boneyards were piles of parts seldom used—beneficial only to the mice who lived there and the snakes that preyed on the mice.

The expectations of a STIHL user have always been much higher than that of other brands. Consequently, technical problems had to be addressed aggressively by STIHL, STIHL American,

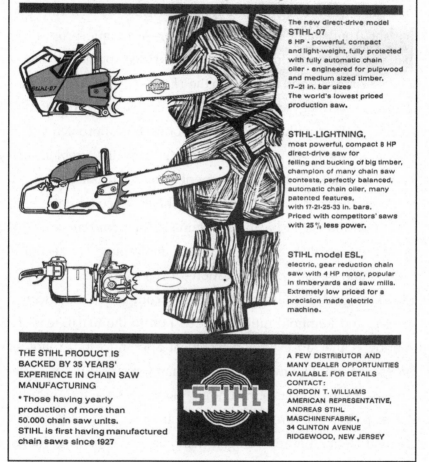
the distributors, and the dealers. One of the reasons for Tull-Williams's financial challenges and the subsequent partnership with the Stihl family—establishing STIHL American—was the short-term and expensive strategy to tackle technical failures of STIHL units in the field. Realizing that technical challenges would

be a mainstay and that identifying the problem and implementation of a solution would require factory participation, Gordon, Andreas, and the STIHL engineers began the development of a long-term technical strategy: identifying the precise problem in the field and testing design-change features to eliminate reasons for failure. The strategy would require STIHL to be a channel participant from manufacturer to end-user—a unique proposition that, years later, would be studied and written about by business school professors and featured in the *The Distribution Trap*. Success of the new strategy depended heavily on the person chosen to go into the field with a specific focus on technical problems. This person would need to be able to understand the problem and learn the culture of the people experiencing the problem.

Andreas's confidant Reinhold Guhl had been keeping his eye on an industrial business administrator's apprentice who'd earned impeccable grades and had an affinity for technical matters and verbal communication—a rare combination. Rainer Gloeckle's grades qualified him for early completion of his formal studies, and Reinhold quickly added him to the STIHL team by offering Rainer an extended technical apprenticeship followed by a seven-month stint with the German forestry division. After working in the forests surrounding Germany's Lake Constance, Rainer passed the forestry exam with high scores and became a certified German Forest Ranger. Reinhold was preparing Rainer for the lifelong, worldwide, diverse career he'd have with STIHL. Reinhold knew the task would require a multitalented, quick-learning, and diverse individual.

Reinhold surmised that the forestry certification would endear Rainer to loggers, and the knowledge of advanced two-cycle theory would enable Rainer to diagnose problems occurring only in the field. Rainer, only twenty-one years old at the time, had high expectations of a career with STIHL, but those expectations didn't include him venturing far from home. Rainer quickly proved Reinhold right and has been credited with two design changes. When Reinhold called Rainer into his office, Rainer was taken aback, frightened, and excited when Reinhold offered him a position beyond his wildest dreams. The only problem was the position was in America.

Rainer, born in 1943 during the height of World War II, never knew his father—a German officer killed January 6, 1945, during the Battle of the Bulge. There was no funeral—as was the case in most instances in those days—just a death notice, long after the fact. It was seven years before the International Red Cross informed Rainer and his mother of the details of his father's, and her husband's, death and the burial site: a military cemetery in Luxemburg. Rainer, like many fatherless German war children, had a deep emotional bond with his mother. He had to confer with her before giving Reinhold an answer. Recognizing the magnitude of the opportunity, she tearfully consented. With his mother's blessing, Rainer accepted the offer.

A week after accepting the position in America, Rainer was packed and ready to go when Reinhold asked if he'd first spend some time in Sweden. Word had gotten around. Wolf Manfred von Richthofen, STIHL's importer for Scandinavia, had heard about Rainer and his technical expertise. Wolf Manfred was the son of Lothar von Richthofen, who was the younger brother to Manfred von Richthofen, the famed World War I German fighter pilot Ace, the Red Baron. It's said that Lothar, having scored more kills in a shorter period of time than the Red Baron and never having been shot down, was most likely a better pilot than his famed, flamboyant older brother. At any rate, Wolf Manfred and his German pedigree had considerably more political clout than Gordon Williams. STIHL American would have to wait.

Sweden, while an important market for STIHL, was comparatively small relative to America, and consequently their technical issues were fewer. Seven months later, Rainer's American work visa had been transferred from the American Embassy in Germany to the Embassy in Sweden. He was approved for work in America. By then, Rainer had learned the Swedish language and had trained technicians throughout Sweden, which would serve him well later. Finished with the task assigned to him by Reinhold, and with nothing further to do but search for Swedish girls suitable for STIHL's infamous calendar, Rainer headed for America, against Wolf Manfred's wishes. Rainer would return to Sweden years later for a different challenge.

Rainer arrived in the United States in July 1964 with a keen grasp of most things technical relating to STIHL and a fluent knowledge of numerous European languages—but not so much English, and certainly not the language spoken in New Jersey. Gordon met Rainer at the same airport—possibly the same international gate where he and Harding had arrived after making the trip to Germany in 1958. By then, New York, in honor of President Kennedy, had changed the name from Idlewild International to JFK International.

Victor Roessler, the first German to be assigned to STIHL American from STIHL Germany and who worked for Harding Smith at STIHL Parts, had been in the United States for over a year by then and offered Rainer a place to live. Victor and Rainer roomed together in Hackensack for several months. Rainer learned the language, which he soon realized was much different than the Queen's English he'd studied in school. Victor and Rainer commuted to work each day in Victor's drab green Volkswagen until Victor returned to Germany. With Gordon's help, Rainer purchased his first car—a 1958 Olds.

STIHL Parts—Early Days. Notice photo of Andreas Stihl—upper left

Victor returned to Germany as soon as he'd finished teaching Rainer the fundamentals of the warehouse. "Rainer," Joe Minarik said, "was not so hot in the warehouse but thought he was God's gift to everyone's daughter." Rainer, as it turns out, was not in his element in the warehouse, but true to his training, was ingenious with regard to technical issues. He was a godsend for those in technical service all across America, and an exemplary ambassador for STIHL.

Joe Minarik—Mock—the independent-thinking, initiative-taking cabinetmaker, was offered a full-time position soon after Victor returned to Germany. Rainer was able to devote his attention to the much-needed technical services. Hiring Joe for the warehouse and allowing Rainer to focus on servicing dealers and distributors was an obvious and easy decision for Gordon. Joe and Evelyn invited Rainer to their home many times for home-cooked meals. Rainer still speaks very highly of Joe, Evelyn, and the Minarik family.

STIHL Parts – Early Days

Once Rainer had mastered the American-English language, or the butchered version spoken in New Jersey, Gordon sent him to Wellington, Ohio, to United Welding for his first distributor visit. Rainer's first trip inside the United States was to visit the first US STIHL distributor established by Gordon, and he would be conducting his first technical service school. It was a first of many. Evidently, all went well. Gordon then sent Rainer to several other distributors throughout the entire United States to do the same. There were no frequent flyer miles in those days, but Rainer was certainly a frequent flyer and logged thousands of miles by bus too.

It was during one of those first trips that Rainer visited my dad, Don Crader, of Crader Distributing in Marble Hill, Missouri, population 450. After his long ride and countless stops on a Continental Trailways bus from Tupelo, Mississippi, Dad, Teri, and I met him at the bus stop. We picked him up in an International Harvester Scout, an early version of today's ubiquitous SUVs and one of Dad's trademarks. At the time, it was Dad's routine to remove the hardtop on the Scout on Memorial Day and drive topless until Labor Day. A poncho was stuffed under each seat. It was a late summer night when Rainer arrived in Marble Hill, and he was the only person to get off the bus. The bus stop was simply the cracked sidewalk in front of a Rexall drugstore. The only vehicle in sight in the sleepy little town was a Scout with no top and a man smoking a Roi-Tan cigar, who was accompanied by two small kids. It was a very unfamiliar scene to a twenty-one-year-old used to a densely populated and heavily regulated, war-torn Germany and, more recently, the fast-paced environs of New Jersey.

County Blessed With Active, Well Equipped Sherrif's Patrol

A GYRO-COPTER - The Patrol expects to receive a gyro-copter in the next few months that will be put to use in air search. Rainer Gloeckle, patrol member will pilot the aircraft.

Rainer Gloeckle and Dad became quick friends. Rainer grew to appreciate and prefer the people and culture of rural America. He found the rural people to be very resourceful and empathetic to the needs of a typical STIHL user. It was during one of his many trips to Crader Distributing that Rainer and Dad developed the first technical bulletin, a document that provided the dealer with a schematic explaining the best technical procedure for adjusting the timing on the model 07 chainsaw. In time the two of them designed bulletins addressing other issues. Design and distribution of technical bulletins was eventually adopted by STIHL American.

Pictured in the photo is Rainer examining a model 07 saw while it is running under a load on a dynamometer rigged up by Don Crader. The dynamometer allowed the saw to be run under a load while in a service shop. During the summer of 1965, the 07 experienced a fuel vapor lock problem, primarily in Missouri. The same problem eventually turned up in other southern states, but by then the problem had been diagnosed and the fix engineered. With the aid of Don's contraption, Rainer was instrumental in diagnosing the problem and the design change. Rainer believes the problem surfaced first at Crader since Crader had sold more saws than any other southern distributor at the time.

Gordon helped Rainer replace his 1958 Olds with a 1960 Cadillac convertible, helped him pack his bags, and saw him off on a road trip all the way across the United States to California. STIHL was beginning to make giant inroads in the West and Northwest. Along with the increase in sales was the increase in need for technical expertise. Rainer relocated to San Leandro, California, where he helped Gordon and Harding establish a West Coast presence. Once established, he spent little time at the ware-

house and continued to travel, primarily in the West but also to all
other points in America, wherever he was of most value.

Rainer traveled extensively throughout the United States
troubleshooting isolated technical issues, training distributor
technicians, and making countless dealer calls. Eventually, the
presentations became a mix of technical and sales training. Rainer
developed a number of clever presentations that demonstrated
STIHL's superiority. When asked why STIHLs developed much
more power per pound than other brands, Rainer explained the
close tolerances of the piston and cylinder, which in some cases
were ten times closer than McCulloch or Homelite. He demonstrated the close tolerances by removing the rings from the piston,
inserting the piston into the cylinder, placing his finger over the
spark plug hole, and holding the assembly out for all to see. The
piston wouldn't drop out until he removed his thumb from the
spark plug hole.

Two STIHL 090s power Rainer's gyrocopter

Another convincing demonstration was to start a saw, lay it upside down, and take bets on how long it would run inverted. Some saws ran for hours before stopping from fuel exhaustion. One of the easiest obstacles he addressed was the concern that STIHL saws were metric. Rainer simply explained that all brands, even Homelite and McCulloch, used metric threads for the spark plug. When asked why, he explained that metric threads were denser than the American standard and, consequently, stronger. Almost instantly, metric threads became a selling feature.

Rainer remained in the United States until 1971, when he was asked to relocate to Scandinavia and assume several responsibilities, including product and business development and distribution of STIHL all across northern Europe. During this time, while serving on Sweden's Forestry Accident Prevention Committee, Rainer was instrumental in the development of STIHL's innovative chain-braking system. Versed in multiple languages and cultures, the whiz kid eventually became STIHL's primary expert witness dealing with product liability.

Deputy Sheriff Rainer on mounted patrol

In January 1966, having traveled ahead of the group, Rainer was eagerly awaiting the STIHL American flight arrival in Germany.

Chapter Thirteen
MAN OF STIHL

THE CAPTAIN AWOKE EVERYONE BY announcing our passing over the White Cliffs of Dover and the beginning of a slow descent into Germany. Everyone awoke except the ones who'd hung around Gordon's table too long. Soon thereafter, we began our descent into Stuttgart. Word made its way through the cabin that a few of the men on board had last seen Germany from the air while aboard a B-17. Margot never promoted it, but by week's end most knew that she'd flown the famed B-17, the "aluminum overcast."

During the descent, Ernie Rainey made his way through the cabin sporting his legendary trademark smile, letting everyone know how passport customs would work, and making sure that everyone was comfortable. His grip swallowed mine when we shook hands. Allow me to introduce Ernie, the first man of STIHL in America.

Roger Maris had recently broken Babe Ruth's home run record, much to the dismay of most Yankee fans; they'd preferred that the record stand, and if it was to be broken, "let Mantle be the one." Cassius Clay, after cruising to the Gold at the 1960 Olympics, was beginning the long-lasting spar with Howard Cosell, the Russians were building a missile base in Cuba, Bob Dylan was inspired to pen the lyrics to "The Times They are A-Changin'," and STIHL American added a superstar.

Years later, when a STIHL salesman walked through a dealer's door, he'd oftentimes be greeted with, "There's the Man of STIHL." A few bolder STIHL salesmen would sign their name with the initials MOS. Of course Andreas Stihl was the first man of STIHL, but in this instance we're talking about the many road warriors who combed the countryside looking for establishments willing to carry STIHL.

Becoming a STIHL dealer in the early days meant displaying a chainsaw or two, selling the only model available, stocking a handful of Fairbanks Morse starter parts, possessing rudimentary technical skills, having an untiring work ethic, and developing a genuine relationship with rugged, no-nonsense loggers. The initial challenge was getting outdoor power equipment distributors to carry STIHL and make them available for sale by their army of territory managers.

Legions of road warriors frequently claim to be the first to have introduced STIHL to a particular region, state, or county in America. For most, STIHL was but a page in a thick overstuffed binder with information about the many vendors they represented. At the time, a sale was a sale, and to sell a chainsaw meant little more than selling a lawn mower or a case of air filters. And for some, selling a German saw posed unnecessary risk. Selling STIHL wouldn't significantly improve take-home pay.

With the financial backing of the Stihl family secured, Gordon and Harding had a second chance at success. Harding's future success selling parts depended on Gordon's success selling saws. Gordon had Harding's support with any strategy to increase saw sales. Gordon, having learned from his earlier experience during the Tull-Williams era, chose a slightly different strategy. With the perfect person in mind to start with, he decided to increase the sales staff.

At that time Gordon, the only salesperson, was spending half his time managing the business part of STIHL American. Gordon's administrative assistant, his wife, Ann, kept the books at home while attending to their two young sons and the apple of his eye, their daughter. So, the addition of a full-time salesperson meant a doubling or quadrupling of the sales efforts for STIHL American; Gordon had no intention of slowing down.

While STIHL was already popular in the heavy-logging parts of the country, Gordon's vision was for STIHL to be sold in all parts of America. Gordon realized it would take a special person to convince regional distributors to carry STIHL, a saw manu-factured in Germany, and to inspire regional salesmen—travel-ing solo throughout the country—to make blind sales calls on small-engine shops, service stations, and rental yards.

It's not known if Gordon wrote the job description for the first STIHL salesman with a particular person in mind or if, with a particular person in mind, he wrote the job description. Based on Gordon's proclivity for loyalty to friends and family, it's likely that he had Ernie Rainey in mind—a childhood friend, high school classmate, and captain of the Ridgewood football team.

After graduation from Ridgewood, Ernie attended the University of New Hampshire (UNH) before serving in the navy as a physical training instructor. After his military service, Ernie he returned to UNH, was student body president, played on the undefeated UNH football team, was inducted into the UNH hall of fame, and married Miss New Hampshire. After graduation from UNH, he was drafted by the New York Giants. He declined the offer because he could make more money selling for Spalding Sporting Goods and working as a lifeguard in New Hampshire during the summer. Professional football was simply a game in those days.

Ernie wasn't particularly tall by today's standards, a little over six feet, but he was a brute of a man, as thick as he was wide with a neck that extended straight below his ears to heavily muscled shoulders. His smile was toothy and genuine, and his laugh could fill a stadium. He had giant, bone-crushing hands, but his handshake was only firm, not painful, and always included a simultaneous backslap. He claimed to do fifty push-ups every morning. Just by looking at him, I'd say he did more like five hundred. Had he gone pro, he could have been a mentor to Dick Butkus.

STIHL Incorporated periodically holds national sales confer-
ences, where salespeople from all over the United States meet.
The introduction usually includes one's name, the distributor
one is working for, and the area one covers. Some in the sparsely
populated West still cover entire states, though most territories
are much smaller, and some cover only a few counties. Ernie,
the predecessor to thousands who would follow and become the
revered Man of STIHL to their dealers, was responsible for the
entire United States, including Alaska and Hawaii. He traveled
millions of miles by car and air, and since hotels were few and far
between in those days, Ernie occasionally slept in airport lounges
or rental cars. He was known to hitchhike when necessary. He
quickly earned the trust and became friends with many distributors established throughout America. He was often invited into
the homes of his customers, STIHL distributors. Whatever story is
told by the men of STIHL today, it's likely that Ernie has been there
and plowed that furrow multiple times long ago.

Much like when they played football at Ridgewood, Ernie and
Gordon were a team; it was oftentimes difficult to know where
one ended and the other began. Gordon would eventually author
a book, *Winning Sales*. Just as with the job description of the first
STIHL salesman in America, it's impossible to know if the book
was written for or inspired by Ernie.

Ernie got everyone on the flight to follow the captain's orders:
take a seat and strap on the seatbelt. Ernie finally settled in while
the landing gear was being extended.

Chapter Fourteen

THE TURM

WE WERE WELCOMED AT STUTTGART's airport by a gaggle of STIHL Germany people including a local oompah band. Since I was seated in the rear of the plane and the last to get off, it seemed like it took longer for people to get off the plane than it did to fly from New York. Several were groggy from the lingering effects of taking something to avoid air sickness, others staggered around after spending too much time at the table, and the rest were growing impatient; I was among the last group.

Our arrival in Germany was 8:00 a.m. local time, and everyone's biological clock was still stateside—roughly 1:00 a.m. It was either too early or too late, definitely too something, to appreciate the gusto of the band. For those who'd lingered too long at the galley table, the band was likely more annoying than fingernails scraping across a blackboard. In spite of a thick overcast sky, many were donning dark sunglasses—mostly hiding puffy, bloodshot eyes from our overly enthusiastic, ready-to-party and gracious German hosts.

The group was too large for a single bus or single hotel, so we were divided according to our Stuttgart destination. Our bus was destined for Stuttgart's Turm Hotel, the same place Gordon and Harding had stayed during their 1958 visit. The historic hotel was dark, cold, and drafty, but everyplace in Germany is dark, cold, and drafty in the winter. The elevator was scarcely large enough for two people and luggage. Dad had read that exercise was the best way to beat jet lag; there was to be no jet lag for the Craders. We lugged our bags up the tiny stairway to the fifth floor, at which inconvenient time I learned that the first floor in Germany is the first floor above the ground floor. We unpacked and left for a short walk down the longest pedestrian street in all of Europe: Stuttgart's famed Koenigstrasse (also the most popular shopping district in Stuttgart). Mom and Dad purchased what was supposed to be my one and only souvenir, a pair of Meindl boots. I own a pair today that, although larger, closely resembles those purchased fifty years ago.

Dinner was quiet. Most of the galley table group didn't show up. Dad whispered to me that he was sure they'd feel like a bag of cow turds come morning. Something in his inflection caused me to believe that his comment was more hopeful than declarative. The exception to the rule was Gene Ahlborn, from Sayner, Wisconsin. Gene was gregariously moving from table to table greeting people; belly laughing and making sure everyone was enjoying themsleves. Gene had that magical, genuine persona that endeared himself to everyone. It was Gene who collaborated with Fred Oswald in getting the Green Bay Packers' Ray Nitschke to pose for a poster holding a STIHL 041AV.

Growing up, I can recall being forced to take a nap. That trip, I'd begged for a nap but was forced to stay awake. When permission finally came, I collapsed on a soft, fluffy, feather-stuffed, quilt-looking thing that I later learned was called a duvet, but that's not the bad part. The duvet that had invited me to enjoy a luxurious sleep was lying atop a mattress that was surely packed with sandstone. "Firm" doesn't come close to describing it. Other than there being no ice cubes in all of Europe, the marble substitute for a mattress was my only disappointment. My body was too exhausted for my jaw to work. I fell asleep without complaining.

Six o'clock in the morning in Germany is already afternoon in most of America. Teri and I headed to the top floor where a deluxe German breakfast buffet was promised to be waiting. Each floor of the hotel consisted of a small square lobby into which all rooms, the elevator, and the stairway opened. Rather than wait on the slow, creepy elevator, we took the stairs. The stairway wrapped around the tiny elevator shaft and opened into the elevator lobby on each floor, requiring us to walk through every floor lobby on our way to the top. We noticed pairs of freshly polished shoes sitting outside most guest-room doors. The tradition in Germany, at the time, was to place shoes outside your door before midnight, and they'd be polished and returned before 6:00 a.m. I was tempted to switch pairs around, but my sister convinced me to leave well enough alone.

My only buffet experience up to that point was for lunch and dinner, which typically consisted of kettle beef, roast beef, chicken, or deep-fried fish. A German breakfast buffet presenta-tion—the centerpiece a partially fileted eel with its pointed, toothy head still attached and a menacing-looking eyeball that seemed to follow me like Rembrandt's Mona Lisa—wasn't what I expected. I suspect the eel, surrounded by an assortment of thinly sliced mys-terious-looking meat, was intended to curb everyone's appetite. The strategy almost worked until I got to the end and smelled the freshly baked bread—eureka!

While loading my plate with bread, butter, and jam, I noticed hard-boiled eggs sitting in a basket that resembled a hen. They were still warm. It's a good thing I had plenty of bread on my plate because when I cracked the first egg, I learned they were not hard-boiled. The attendant, who I'd decided was mute, snorted, and then brought to the table a single egg holder and a tiny spoon and demonstrated how to slice off the top of the egg's shell. Then he pointed at the top of the egg with the miniature spoon. No words were spoken, but I got the message and, thereafter, was an expert on the not-so-hard-boiled eggs, soon to be known as soft boiled. Who would have known? After watching me consume several slices of bread and go back a couple of times for more eggs, the attendant brought me a thimble-sized glass of orange juice that looked more pink than orange. When I tossed it back like I'd seen the men do schnapps the night before, I discovered that it was in fact grapefruit juice. I chased the bitter surprise with a bite of the roll that had a titanium crust but a velvety inside.

By the time Mom and Dad arrived, Teri and I had identified everything that was safe to eat. The man who'd greeted me with a grimace during my first trip to the eel viewing and instructed me on the finer points of egg eating, brought two miniature cups of extra-strong coffee to the table. Just like the supposed orange juice, the cups were small, but judging by Mom's face when she took a sip, the tiny cup was going to be plenty.

Teri and I looked out the panoramic windows into the dark, snowy abyss that was Stuttgart on a cold January morning before sunrise. A few others trickled in; nobody ate the eel. None of the men who'd been so lively while gorging themselves with Bavarian kerosene the night before were among the early risers, except for Gene Ahlborn.

Gene made his way through the room repeating, *guten morgen* at each table. He paused at ours. "Good-looking family, Donnie." The only other person I'd heard call my dad Donnie was my grandmother.

Dad smiled, "Thanks, Gene." I could tell Dad liked Gene. Maybe it was because, like us, he was from the Midwest. Gene generally behaved in such a way that most people don't appreciate—loud, invading one's personal space—but Gene had a magical charisma. When Gene moved toward the buffet, Dad whispered, "That guy has an iron stomach."

Ahlborn Equipment of Sayner, Wisconsin, began distributing STIHL in 1961, covering Wisconsin, Minnesota, Iowa, and Michigan's Upper Peninsula. Led by company owner Gene Ahlborn—a true dynamo, selling over 1,500 saws in 1965—it was the largest STIHL distributor in the United States at the time. Gene, known to possess an endless source of energy, set an example for thousands. He was an accomplished private pilot, consummate outdoorsman, and once set a sawing record for the six-cubic-inch category at the Great Lakes Forestry Exhibition using a STIHL Super Lightning. His only serious competition at the exhibition was generally the STIHL distributor from Michigan, Tony Ball, another larger-than-life STIHL pioneer.

On the way out, I noticed that Gene had taken a large chunk of the eel and several pieces of the other unidentifiable meat. Dad was right; Gene obviously had an iron stomach.

Chapter Fifteen

BIST DU VERRÜCKT?

GIVEN NO CHOICE IN THE matter, I stayed behind when the men left for the factory tour. While standing in the lobby, I forlornly watched while the businessmen filed out of the Turm into the snowy German morning toward a waiting bus. I was longing to be a businessman when Gene patted me on the shoulder. "Take care of the women today, little Donnie," he said and then let go a Gene Ahlborn trademark laugh. "You'll have a better time than we will," he said. Somehow, he made me believe I would.

The lady's bus made for the Black Forest. Most enjoyed the scenic drive on the winding road through the snow-covered, dense pine forest; a few took turns in the small toilet at the rear of the bus. Peter Stihl's sister, Gerhild, was our tour guide and explained the many points of interest we could have seen if it hadn't been snowing so hard.

Our planned hour-and-a-half drive took over two hours, but once the ladies set their eyes on little, snowy, picturesque Titisee—a lakeside southwestern German village famous for cuckoo clocks—they forgot how long it had taken to get there. Suddenly aware of the opportunity to shop, they were magically infused with adrenaline, unique to the gender, and enthusiastically launched from the bus like a bunch of grade school kids headed for a Dairy Queen. The village was essentially one street with more shops than one could visit in a single day. The shop owners did well that day. I hung around with Gerhild and learned another useful German phrase: *bist du verrückt (you must be crazy)*?

A sense of starvation among the women, due to not getting up in time for breakfast and the promise of lunch, was the only force strong enough to cause them to return to the bus. Lunch was a glamorous affair—each place setting included enough utensils to arm an entire Midwestern family. Teri and I had been instructed on what to expect and knew to use the outside pieces first. One of the ladies mentioned that it was after five in the afternoon in America, and with that observation they all began to enjoy the fine German wine to the extreme. Everyone slept during the return trip to the hotel; that's when I learned that some women can snore like a man.

Chapter Sixteen

THE CHIEF

THAT NIGHT WE WALKED TO a lively downstairs restaurant just off Koenigstrasse. Even though it was a private dinner, the seating and service was chaotic. A band with buxom women, unnecessarily wearing push-up bras, and men in leather shorts, even though it was January, kept the mood festive. The band got more than they bargained for when they began to pick people from the audience to bring up on stage and chose Chief Jack Beatty. It was likely the Indian headband he'd worn that got the band's attention.

Chief Beatty stole the show by performing a couple of traditional Osage dances that included singing in his Native Osage language. Germans love everything about the western United States. They are particularly intrigued with anything having to do with cowboys and Indians. Chief Beatty got a standing ovation, and many throughout the restaurant sent steins of beer to his table. Since he didn't drink, the complimentary beers were of benefit to everyone at his table except him and his wife. In spite of never drinking and a difficult past, Chief Beatty was always smiling.

Four Osage men with US President Calvin Coolidge after signing the Indian Citizenship Act of 1924, which granted Native Americans across the country full citizenship for the first time. (Source — LOC, LC-USZ62-111409 DLC.)

Rainer with Mr. and Mrs. Jack (Chief) Beatty

As was the case with most Native American tribes, the Osage suffered countless broken promises by the American government. However, unlike most tribes, by the time the Osage were forced to resettle in Oklahoma, they had the financial wherewithal to purchase the ground upon which their reservation was located. Much of this wealth was gained as a result of being paid by the federal government for the land they'd been forced to vacate in Missouri and Kansas. The Osage reservation was comprised of what is now Osage County, Oklahoma.

The discovery of oil in Osage County and the growing need for oil changed everything, and not necessarily for the good. During the early part of the twentieth century, Oklahoma was the largest oil-producing region in the United States. The Osage, owning their land and consequently the mineral rights, became some of the wealthiest people in Oklahoma.

In 1907, as part of the process in preparing Oklahoma for statehood, the federal government allotted 657 acres to each Osage on the tribal rolls. Thereafter, each Osage and that person's legal heirs, whether Osage or not, had headrights to royalties in oil production. This turned out to be a recipe for disaster.

By 1920 the demand for oil had grown such that Osage County began to grow exponentially and became a mecca for illegitimate entrepreneurs, illicit opportunists, and criminals. In 1921, in an effort to protect the Osage from unscrupulous outsiders, the federal government passed a law requiring Osage of half-blood or more in ancestry to have guardians appointed until they demonstrated competency. Most of the guardians were appointed from among newly arrived white lawyers and businessmen. At the time more than eighty lawyers were living in Pawhuska, the Osage County seat, which had only eight thousand residents.

Although the intentions were good, the result became known as the Reign of Terror on the Osage reservation. Since guardians stood to inherit the headrights of their charges, the temptation was too great for a few. After being alerted by the Osage tribal council, the newly formed FBI began its first major murder investigation. It's estimated that by 1925 over sixty wealthy Osage had been killed by murderers for hire.

It wasn't until 1926 that the FBI uncovered an elaborate scheme of a well-known and powerful rancher who tried to gain control of a large block of Osage land. He'd arranged for his nephew to marry into the tribe and then systematically had several members of his nephew's wife's family murdered. The murderer was allegedly a convicted burglar who was regularly released from jail late at night by bribed guards to commit the murders and then return to jail with an alibi.

In 1925 Congress passed a law prohibiting inheritance of headrights by non-natives of Osage ancestry, which all but eliminated the Reign of Terror.

After a three-year investigation, one person was sentenced to life in prison for his role in the murders. At the objection of the Osage Nation, he was paroled in 1959 and, in 1965, granted a full pardon. The Osage Nation was required to pay the FBI for the cost of the investigation.

Jack (Chief) Beatty, born in Oklahoma to an Osage Indian chief, was orphaned at four. His appointed guardians moved with Jack to Denver, Colorado, where he came of age and retained his headrights. Little is known about Chief Beatty's parents or the circumstances of their deaths. It's possible that both parents died of natural causes, but it's likely that there's a more sordid explanation.

Chief Beatty was one of the earliest adopters of STIHL, coming on board with Tull-Williams in 1958. When asked why he chose STIHL, Chief Beatty replied, "Because they're made with precision and are trouble free." The chief's area of responsibility included: Colorado, New Mexico, Wyoming, Eastern Montana, and the Oklahoma panhandle. His territory stretched from Glacier National Park almost all the way to Amarillo, Texas, a distance of nearly fifteen hundred miles by car.

Rainer Gloeckle recalls traveling with Chief Beatty during the early days. The chief always drove a Chrysler New Yorker, and Rainer was intrigued with the push-button automatic transmission of the Chrysler. Rainer regularly flew into Denver Stapleton where Chief Beatty would be waiting with his New Yorker packed to the gills with gifts, saws, and a list of dealers who'd been experiencing technical problems. They'd spend the week calling on dealers, handling technical issues, delivering a saw to those with urgent need, and taking orders.

Chief Beatty and his wife had a beautiful home in Denver with an ample three-car garage where two cars were parked alongside an inventory of STIHL saws and parts. After each week of traveling the territory, visiting dealers and taking orders, the chief pulled parts from meticulously organized shelves, packaged them, and then delivered them to the post office for shipment. His was a true one-man operation. In most cases, saw orders were shipped from the garage supply. Chief Beatty also had saws shipped directly from STIHL American's warehouse in New Jersey, by way of the Trailways bus service, to the remotely located dealers. It was the least expensive and quickest way to ship a single chainsaw to an isolated location. And, in those days, anything west of the Mississippi was considered remote.

Each week's travel included several stops at the various Indian reservations in Chief's territory, where he'd hand out gifts for the less fortunate. Rainer frequently saw him giving people money after making them promise they'd spend it on food rather than liquor. The chief was highly respected throughout the territory; his endorsement was enough for most, so his endorsement of STIHL was of considerable value.

During his tenure as STIHL's distributor for most of the Rockies, Chief exclusively sold the STIHL Lightning. The higher elevation required more power, and since the Lightning was relatively light, the chief saw no reason to confuse people with multiple models, some of which wouldn't perform well at high altitude. Offering one model made management of the garage-housed parts and saw inventory more efficient.

One downside to offering a limited selection of models is that when a technical problem occurs, it's likely to affect every customer, which is precisely what happened. During a couple of swings through the territory, Chief heard numerous complaints about the inconsistency of the power of Super Lightnings; one saw would have plenty of power while another identical saw would not. Chief called the whiz kid.

Within days Rainer and the chief were heading into the Black Hills of Wyoming, the hotspot of the problems, where the most recent shipment of new Super Lightnings had been sent. After fuel system pressure testing a selection of saws and experiencing no problems and then testing an equal number of those that had experienced power loss, Rainer easily diagnosed that the problem was in the carburetor. He discovered that the saws that weren't experiencing power loss all had the same diaphragm metering spring, while the problem saws had a variety of springs of a different tension and alloy.

While testing the carburetors, Rainer also used his special tools to check the ignition timing of each saw. While doing so he taught both the dealers and Chief the value of special tools. The chief was so impressed that he subsequently began teaching the dealers the value of proper technical-problem diagnosing through the use of special tools, and was possibly the first distributor to do so.

The carburetor company was delighted to hear from Rainer regarding the inconsistency of their metering springs; they'd been hearing sporadic complaints of the same issue with other brands of saws and other types of products used at high elevation.

The chief rewarded Rainer for his quick response and solution with a trip through nearby Yellowstone National Park where Rainer saw, for the first time, grizzly bears, buffalos, and of course Old Faithful.

Future-focused, rich with optimism, and always sporting a toothy smile, the chief never spoke of his past or the mistreatment of the Osage.

Chapter Seventeen

THE FORTIETH
ANNIVERSARY SAW

ON OUR LAST NIGHT IN Germany, we were treated to a ballroom gala along with several people from the factory. Numerous toasts were hoisted—for what, I don't recall. I was too busy counting the silverware and stemmed crystal glasses of all shapes and sizes. The highlight of the evening was Hans Peter Stihl unveiling the STIHL model 040, in celebration of STIHL's fortieth year. As it turned out, the invitation to the trip was accompanied with a commitment to purchase a minimum quantity of 040s. Dad's commitment of two hundred seemed monumental at the time.

Breakfast the next morning was as interesting as the first morning. Too many had used every utensil the previous night and had made a futile effort to empty every wine glass, each of which was quickly but stealthily topped off by a nearby waiter who'd evidently been given an incentive to empty as many bottles of wine as possible into the dizzy Americans.

Again, I watched the men board the buses for the factory. I didn't know it then, but I'd be working at the STIHL factory eight years later.

The women were free to do as they pleased. Gerhild offered to show them the best shops on the Koenigstrasse, which by that time I was convinced stretched all the way to China. In fact, the street ended at Schlossplatz—German for "castle place"—said to be the largest square in Stuttgart. It is a wide-open area surrounded by an ornate building named Neues Schloss, which means "new castle," and is aptly named since it's only a couple hundred years old—new by European standards.

Mom, Teri, and I walked the entire length of the famed Koenigstrasse just to say we did, I suppose. On the way back, we stepped into a shop Gerhild highly recommended, one specializing in Hummel figurines. At lunch Mom and Teri described their purchases in excruciating detail. The surrounding women gobbled up their lunch and rushed off to seek their Hummel treasure.

To the men's dismay, they returned from the factory in time to be force marched down Koenigstrasse to shops in which the women had seen items too expensive to purchase without first convincing the husbands of the great need for said item. Mom took Dad to a shop selling Dresden Ambrosius Lamm tableware. Since she'd been doing all the bookkeeping for the business their entire marriage and was yet to be paid "one red cent"—I think is how she posited it—she felt deserving. Dad acquiesced, which Teri and I thought odd, since our dining table had only two chairs, and it had never been used for anything other than neatly stacked piles of invoices, receipts, and ledger books. Dad used his new Diners Club credit card to pay for the dishes and had them shipped home. Luckily, the charges never appeared on his statement. In spite of contacting Diners Club by phone and the shop by mail, he was never charged. The cost of the complete set of dishes and serving pieces had exceeded the cost of the entire trip for the four of us. It would be several years before Mom had a house big enough for a china cabinet. Until then the dishes remained stored in boxes.

Chapter Eighteen

THE SPEECH

THROUGHOUT THE MEETING COUNTLESS STIHL stories were shared. Few were new but, given enough German wine, every story new or old was tolerated, if not appreciated. One such story that has been handed down is known as "The Speech," which had occurred during the Tull-Williams era.

The STIHL D24 Super Lightning, also referred to as the Contra, was a magnificent machine—light, fast, and relative to other brands, dependable—at least that's how they are remembered. Early STIHL owners, much like dogmatic Harley owners, are sometimes given to a memory that simultaneously exaggerates and diminishes facts. That is, the good is amplified marginally beyond reality and the bad is expunged.

Nearly all brands of saws of the Super Lightning era had perpetual technical problems. Taking the saw to the log meant taking an internal combustion engine to filthy operating conditions, and running the saws in all positions. Naturally, there was demand for more power, which resulted in exceeding the limits and engine fatigue. New crankcase designs were rapidly developed and tested. Running the saws in all positions required a new kind of carburetor, one dependent on vacuum rather than gravity. The powerful engines required carburetors that could govern the speed of the engine in order to keep the operator safe and not over-rev and ruin the engine.

A few Super Lightning saws remain in running condition today and are prized by their original owners. Some have been handed down through the generations. Most stories told by owners or heirs are of the day the saw was purchased. They speak reverently of the first STIHL in the family, how proud they are, how the saw never gave them a lick of trouble, and how the saw was the envy of the loggers. Many boast that their purchase was the first STIHL sale for the local STIHL dealer. All of what is said is told as truth; some of it is. The only thing we know for sure is that at one point every dealer sold their first STIHL, and now hundreds claim to own the first STIHL sold.

A sale is the goal, but the more numerous the sales of an imperfect product, the more widespread the problems. The Super Lightning was winning county fair sawing competitions coast to coast. The popularity of the STIHL, in spite of the technical problems associated with housing and unreliable carburetion, had distributors flummoxed. Tull-Williams continued to provide product, distributors continued to sell; both success and problems grew exponentially. This all came to a head at a conference and a legendary keynote comment.

Reinhold Guhl, export manager and fluent in English, attended all meetings alongside Andreas Stihl, who was never interested in learning English. Reinhold, at first glance, appeared to be the quintessential old-school German: firm and void of small talk or pointless humor. He was always smoking a cigarette while peering over thick-lensed bifocals. His smile appeared to be more one of clever and sinister bemusement, rather than recognition of humor. However, Reinhold projected a persona that conflicted with his typical behavior. I'll share two stories to explain.

While working at the STIHL factory in Germany during the

summer of 1974, I had the privilege of sharing a lunch with Reinhold. To this day the STIHL executives routinely join the employees in the factory canteen for lunch. While they usually sit at a reserved table, the family regularly mixes with hourly, salaried, young, and old on a daily basis. Reinhold, remembering that I was the son of an American distributor, took a seat next to me one day and—just after I'd taken a ravenous bite of sauerbraten—asked about American music and what I preferred.

I assumed he preferred the classical composers such as Mozart, Bach, Brahms, Straus, Chopin, and other composers who wrote music with no lyrics. Therefore, coming up with someone comparable and truly American had me stumped. Given more time I would have replied Mancini or Gershwin; I didn't. After thinking long and hard, or until I'd swallowed the sauerbraten, I decided on who I thought was a true American composer—Johnny Horton. Reinhold and I were the only people at the table speaking English. I went on to mention others, such as Hank Williams and Johnny Cash, but Reinhold was most impressed with Horton, my first recommendation. He shocked me by asking that I send him a Jonathon Horton cassette. Soon after returning to America, I sent him a *Johnny Horton's Greatest Hits* cassette, and I expected that to be the end of it.

Several years later, while attending a STIHL meeting in Florida, my wife and I had the privilege of sitting with Reinhold for breakfast. While smoking a strong-odor-emitting cigarette, he gazed skyward—we were outside, thank goodness—struck a pondering pose, and told the table about the American composer I'd recommended to him, a Mr. Jonathon Horton. Between long drags on his cigarette, Reinhold told of his favorite Horton song, the one that featured a fantastic battle in New Orleans, one in which the

Americans defeated the British by using an alligator as a cannon. I nearly choked on my pancake. He never broke a devious smile during the explanation and looked to be in deep, contemplative thought—serious and appreciative. Looking back, Henry Mancini may have been a more appropriate suggestion, but I went with what I knew, and it worked out.

This next example causes one to wonder how much translational assistance Reinhold provided during the introductory 1958 meeting between Andreas Stihl, Gordon, and Harding. Many who heard the legendary speech have attested to Reinhold's international diplomatic skills. The annual distributor meeting occurred in the midst of the technical problems with the Super Lightning. During the meeting Andreas witnessed distributors congratulating themselves on great sales successes but then complaining to him, through Reinhold, about the technical problems and frequent product and parts shortages at Tull-Williams.

Since the wives had been invited to the meeting, a concluding gala dinner was planned. Andreas was the keynote speaker; his speeches were never long and rarely written down, more of a keynote statement than a speech. It was expected he'd say a few congratulatory words regarding the tremendous sales achieved by the American distributors. As usual, Reinhold was the interpreter.

The speech has been shared with me by multiple eyewitness sources. While the wording is a little different, depending on the source, the gist of the speech is consistent. A number of Americans present understood enough German to know what was said; their versions vary, but only slightly. Recently, through email with Reinhold's granddaughter, Reinhold validated the following.

Earlier that day, Mr. Andreas Stihl had met with the distributors and—rather than receive wondrous accolades for the powerful D24 Contra—he'd fielded, through Reinhold translating, countless complaints regarding all the technical problems. The distributors, not yet versed on strict German protocol and the appropriate timing of complaints, held nothing back. Andreas would have the last word, or so he thought.

When the time came for Andreas to address the gala crowd, he approached the podium and, without notes, said the following in German, with rapt enthusiasm: "I am surrounded by nobodies. I should throw you all out and hire new people from the street. At least they will do what I tell them. If things continue like this, it is probably best for me to sell the whole business to McCulloch."

Reinhold, realizing that everyone understood the name McCulloch, interpreted the announcement as follows: "Welcome and thank you for coming. With good products and excellent distributors like you, one day we will even beat McCulloch."

Andreas received a thunderous applause and standing ovation. It's not known if he realized Reinhold's clever deception, but the audience's response set him on a course to make the needed changes. STIHL replaced the sand-cast molds with the much more expensive but precise die-cast. They leaned on the carburetor vendor, and carburetors were improved. STIHL eventually purchased a carburetor manufacturer. And possibly the most strategically impactful move, STIHL made a significant investment in the United States by helping capitalize STIHL American, and so enjoyed a 300 percent sales increase the following year.

It's always interesting to ponder what would have happened if the United States had not defeated the British. What would have happened had Reinhold not revised the legendary speech? Things would have certainly been different. It's not known if

Andreas ever learned of the intentional misinterpretation or if, in fact, he and Reinhold had cooked up the routine simply to send a message. Legend has it that Andreas never knew, and that makes for a better story. One thing is certain: STIHL continued to improve on an already superior product and stayed true to the channel strategy most beneficial to the customer.

It was that day that Andreas got in the last word and Reinhold saved the distributors and inadvertently set the course for STIHL's preeminence in North America.

Chapter Nineteen
LE GAY PAREE

WE WERE LEAVING EARLY THE next morning to head by train to Paris, so each group met for an early dinner at their respective hotels. Inter-table conversation was vigorous—men telling each other what they'd seen, even though they'd all seen the same thing, and women waiting for other women to stop talking so they could tell about their special purchase of the day.

Only twenty years had passed since World War II, and there remained countless signs of heavy-arms battle all the way from Stuttgart to Paris. The train right-of-way paralleled the Maginot line for a few miles, giving everyone a chance to see the exposed tops of a few abandoned bunkers.

Fred Whitson, the STIHL distributor for Tennessee, closely surveyed the landscape from Stuttgart to Paris. He'd seen much of it twenty years earlier from the deck of a Sherman tank.

Fred, born 1920, came of age in the hardscrabble Appalachian environs of western North Carolina, just east of the rugged part of the United States that gave us World War I hero Sergeant York, and south of the coal mining country that produced World War II hero Chuck Yeager. In a material sense, one might think he didn't have much, but in a better fount of lucidity, one would realize he had everything: a practical and impeccable sagacity of ethics and values. Thousands, sporting sneakers that likely cost more than Fred's first car, now plod through his childhood stomping grounds on a trail that gourmet-coffee and espresso sippers at a nearby Starbucks refer to as the AT—identified on hiking maps as the Appalachian Trail.

While coming of age, Fred spent plenty of days in the woods but rather than mindlessly wandering around, he was getting an education that would prepare him well for when he'd eventually become one of STIHL American's earlier distributors. Fred's educational foundation was sufficient at age fourteen when during the depths of the Great Depression, he left the confines of the classroom behind to begin farming and logging in order to support his mother, three younger siblings, and eventually, a brood of seven.

Like so many of his kind, soon after that infamous day in December 1941, Fred enlisted in the army. He spent nearly four years of the War chasing Germany's famed General Rommel throughout Europe while serving in the tank-destroying second infantry division. After participating in the greatest war then known to mankind, Fred returned to the Appalachian hills he called home and picked up where he'd left off—working in the woods, logging, and lumbering.

Shell Station where Fred first repaired saws

The net effect of war is destruction of man, materiel, and matter. Once wars are settled, the restoration begins. The American economy flourished during the years following World War II, and the able-bodied survivors tended to apply skills they'd learned during the war to make a better life for themselves and their families. Having spent roughly 20 percent of their life fighting the Great War, and seeing many lose theirs, they awoke each day with a clear sense of purpose to make up for lost time. For millions of World War II veterans, the war experience had indelibly instilled in them the realization that each day was a blessed gift. They didn't chase a dream; they created it.

Fred (right) listens to a sales pitch

Fred married Jackie, started a family, and applied the skills he'd learned while logging before the war—and those he'd learned working on tanks during the war. Naturally drawn to timber, Fred resumed logging. When crosscut saws gave way to gasoline-powered tree-felling machines, or chainsaws, Fred's wartime experience gave him an advantage. Early chainsaws were handy when they were running but worthless when they weren't, and poorly maintained engines running near the ground in hot, dusty conditions frequently failed. Since Fred had repaired tanks, working on saws was a walk in the park. He quickly gained a reputation for fixing saws.

Jackie

When a representative for the Joe H Brady Company of Birmingham, Alabama—the regional distributor for McCulloch—came looking for a dealer to establish selling chainsaws, he asked who in the area was the best chainsaw repairman. Their research took them to Johnson City, Tennessee, to Fred, who had rented a single bay in a Shell filling station in which he repaired saws of all makes and models. The year was 1953. After purchasing three McCulloch saws and two one-hundred-foot rolls of saw chain, Fred became the area's first chainsaw dealer.

Fred's reputation for repair gained momentum, which led to sales of new saws, which led to the need to formalize and organize. His wife, Jackie, agreed to keep the books and pay the bills while keeping an eye on then six-year-old little Fred. The operation needed a name: Power Tool Company seemed to make sense.

By 1956 Power Tool outgrew the filling station bay and moved into a location of its own, a small building with a giant plate-glass window to display new saws and a large shop to continue the repair and customer support. Small engines continued to make life simpler for all. Lawnmowers with deck-mounted engines began replacing reel mowers. Lawnmower distributors, asking the same questions asked by Joe H Brady Company, got the same answer; Fred began selling lawnmowers, and in 1958 he moved again, this time to a location with more room.

In those days small lawnmower engines were in need of frequent repair. The term shade-tree mechanic was coined when numerous small repair shops cropped up, frequently in a residential garage, where some of the repairs were literally performed beneath the shade of a giant oak. The need for spare parts was such that engine manufacturers began to scurry to find ways to provide parts service to this vast array of repair shops. Fred first ventured into the distribution business by providing spare parts to the many small repair shops sprinkled throughout Appalachia.

It was then that Fred and Jackie learned about wholesale inventory management, shipping, receiving, and — most critical — credit and collections.

Fred and Jackie's experience would serve them well when in 1963 a hard-earned and well-deserved opportunity knocked. After committing to the purchase of forty STIHL chainsaws, Power Tool Company became the exclusive distributor for STIHL American for the entire state of Tennessee. Once again, they would need a bigger building. In 1965 Fred built a new six-thousand-square-foot building with a beautiful showroom and a highly efficient repair facility. He and Jackie were living the dream and building it for another, the next Fred, by then a senior in high school.

Introduction of a German-made saw to the hardened loggers of Appalachia, many of whom had served in Europe during World War II, could have only been possible by one who also had served. One saw at a time, Fred was able to convince loggers to give the STIHL a try. Based on his reputation for service, both in the army and repairing small engines, and the quality of the STIHL product, Fred enabled STIHL to become the preferred saw of the professional logger, but it didn't happen overnight.

Power Tool no longer sells Stihl but as of this writing occupies a 90,000 square-foot facility—their success in the power tool business continues.

We arrived in Paris late in the afternoon, and the entire group fit into one grand hotel. The hotel management seemed delighted to see us arrive and even happier to see us leave.

While in Paris the group was treated to a tour of the city, including the Louvre, Eiffel Tower, Notre Dame Cathedral, Sacre-Couer Basilica, and the Arch de Triumph.

The Louvre is a really cool place for those who are fond of old stuff, giant paintings, and statues of naked people with missing limbs and contorted faces. I wouldn't recommend it if you're allergic to mold and mildew.

In person, the Eiffel Tower looks just like it does in the movies. The French may think their excrement doesn't stink, and maybe it doesn't, but their pigeon crap does; keep your hands off the guardrails on the observatory unless you want a gooey surprise.

I looked for, but never got a glimpse of, the hunchback while touring Notre Dame Cathedral. Taking nearly two hundred years to complete, the place is cavernous, magnificent, and creepy all at once. The roof gutter system is a network of channels that feed into countless rainwater spewing stone gargoyles.

The night before our departure for home, we were treated to a dinner show: a Paris cabaret. To my surprise part of the show included a chorus line of topless dancers, each with a pair of breasts of identical shape and size. That sight, another first for me, was more astonishing than the breakfast eel. No matter, it was late, and I fell asleep, which I'm told entertained almost as many as the bouncing breasts.

On the morning of departure, the hotel lobby was a flurry of activity. For the ladies, reserved chin dipping was replaced with robust full-body hugs, lingering, gentle handshakes, and the exchanging of mailing addresses and phone numbers. The unanimous consensus was they'd just been on the trip of a lifetime. As it turned out, STIHL would go on to host many such celebratory trips for distributors and eventually offer similar, but scaled down, versions for dealers. The future was brighter than anyone could have imagined.

Chapter Twenty

THE PIANO MAN

DURING THE FLIGHT HOME, I tried to process all that I'd seen and experienced; it was too much for a ten-year-old to comprehend. With each following year, my spectator role evolved until I was an active participant. During the summer of 1971, I began getting paid to repair saws—my first major repair being the replacement of the O-ring on the oil pump of an 040. I remember a logger telling me I was "windy" when I told him I'd been to the STIHL factory. I continued to learn; I had the greatest mentor a boy could wish for: Dad, to me and Don, and to everyone else.

Dad's mother, Leora Back (Bach) was born in 1912 at the home of her parents near Zalma, Missouri. She was one of eight children, four boys and four girls. Seven of the children graduated from the eighth grade from Zalma. One brother died at a young age a few days after falling into a boiling kettle of lye.

Leora's parents never owned a motorized vehicle. Their farm was four miles from town going one way and four miles from Berong Baptist Church the other. They'd all ride on a wagon pulled by a team of horses to both places at least once per week, sometimes more often if a fair or special event was taking place in town or a revival at church. The boys left home immediately after graduating from eighth grade and found work in the Saint Louis area. The girls remained on the farm assisting with chores until they married.

Buford Kaiser was born in 1908 near Apple Creek, Missouri—the third of eight children, seven of whom grew to adulthood. An older sister, the only girl in the brood, died of disease at the age of two. Buford's family moved frequently, chasing work. German names were unpopular during World War I: an impediment to finding good work and oftentimes a threat to children at school. They were living in northeast Kansas during the war when Andrew, Buford's father, changed the family name from Kaiser to Crader, taking his wife's maiden name.

Years later, the Craders, still German but with a different name, were living on a farm a few miles outside of Zalma, Missouri, near the home of Leora Back, during Buford's school years. After graduating from eighth grade, the highest grade provided at Zalma, Buford followed his older brother to Saint Louis and found work. The two of them eventually started a small business repairing tires.

Leora, the neighbor farm girl, had caught Buford's eye, and the two exchanged letters. He returned to the area by train and foot several times per year to see Leora. When Leora turned sixteen, her father gave her hand in marriage to Buford. During the summer of 1928, in a hurry to get married, and since Buford was needing to return to Saint Louis for work, they agreed to marry the following day. They preferred a church ceremony at Berong Baptist Church, but the preacher was busy during the week working in the timber woods making railroad ties, a mainstay for the Zalma area. So, Buford picked up Leora at her parents' home using a car borrowed from his older brother, Giff, and they drove to Marble Hill, the county seat, where they were joined in marriage by a justice of the peace. Their honeymoon was the six-hour drive to Saint Louis. It was the first time Leora had been more than twenty miles from home.

Buford and Leora lived in a one-room apartment near the tire store in what is now the south side of Saint Louis. Their first son died at birth. Soon after, they moved to a nearby two-room apartment, purchased their first family Bible, and paid for it over time, twenty-five cents per week. A second son, Donald Dee (Donnie) — my dad — was born in 1933 at the nearby Saint Louis City Hospital. Donald got a sister in 1937 and another in 1938.

In 1944, Buford, never having felt comfortable living in the city and growing weary of the increasing crime in the neighborhood, sold his interest in the tire business to his brother and moved to a farm in Bollinger County, Missouri, just outside of Marble Hill. Buford, with Leora's brother-in-law, and her uncle, pooled their resources and opened Bollinger County Equipment. They began selling International Harvester farm machinery. Donald Dee, then twelve, ran the farm, taking care of livestock, mowing hay, and twice daily milking their one dairy cow.

Leora was hemming a dress and listening to the radio one Saturday afternoon when the phone rang two shorts and a long. The Crader home's party-line ring; it was a friend. "Donnie just won the talent contest," the friend told her.

"What talent contest?" Leora asked. The friend went on to explain that there'd been a talent contest to raise money to finance a building for International Shoe Company—which had promised to locate a shoe factory in Marble Hill if the city provided them a facility. "What in blue blazes did he do to win?" Leora asked.

"Well, he played the piano, of course," the friend answered. "He's a marvelous piano player," she continued.

Leora didn't let the friend know that she had no idea Donnie could play the piano; there wasn't one in the home. Donnie had some explaining to do. Over dinner that night, Donnie explained that he'd been playing the piano at a local tavern. He'd heard and watched another man playing the piano at the tavern during his paper route stops and had been paying close attention to the piano player at church. One day he sat down and started playing.

"It's really not that difficult, Mom," he tried to explain. "The keyboard is divided into little groups of keys that make the same notes only with a little different pitch. I just listen to the music and then find the right group of keys that sound like what I've heard." To Donnie, playing the piano came almost as easy as using one's hands to do figuring. After all, he was half Bach.

Eventually, the obvious conclusion was that he'd been gifted by God to play the piano. During the course of his life, he'd play in countless venues—weddings, church services, funerals, and plays. If a hotel lobby had a piano and Dad had the time, he'd sit down and draw a crowd. Once while touring Germany on a trip to STIHL and having dinner in a Bavarian pub, he asked if he could play the piano when the band took a break. The band never returned from break; the pub was soon overflowing, and pass-ersby crowded around the open windows listening and singing along. He never learned to read music.

Buford replenishing the gasket drawer

By fourteen Donnie—only referred to as Donald Dee by his mother when in trouble—had a part-time job working for his grandfather, Andrew Crader, who by then had settled for good in Bollinger County and owned a Kaiser-Frazer automobile deal-ership. Dad, full of confidence and familiar with Saint Louis, having lived there until eleven, would take the bus from Marble Hill to Saint Louis, pick up new Kaiser-Frazers, and drive them to Marble Hill.

Kasier-Frazers—built in Willow Run, Michigan, in what was

then the largest building in the world, once used to build B24s during World War II—were the best-selling cars in the United States for a few years following the war. By the time Dad turned sixteen, old enough to get a driver's license, he'd been driving for two years.

After graduating from high school in 1951, Dad attended college for one year and then returned home and joined his father, Buford, at Bollinger County Equipment. During the summer of 1952, the two of them bought out the partners and renamed the company Crader Equipment Company, selling International Harvester farm equipment and refrigerators. Dad married his high school sweetheart, Nancy Dewitt. It was an eventful summer for a nineteen-year-old.

Don with his trademark pipe

Dad and Mom signed for their first mortgage, purchasing a two-room, four-hundred-square-foot home for $1,200. Their first child, Teri, a daughter, arrived eleven months later. Fifteen months later, yours truly came along. They arranged a second loan on the house and doubled its size to nearly nine hundred square feet by adding three small bedrooms, an indoor toilet, and central heat. The central heat was essentially a floor furnace located in the center of the house. The dining area was tiny, and the small chrome-sided Formica dinette table had only two vinyl chairs, making room for an upright piano.

Our family gathered for meals around a small bar that separated the kitchen from the would-be dining area. After dinner, Teri and I washed the dishes and cleaned the kitchen while Mom did the books for Crader Equipment and Dad entertained us by playing the piano. His nightly repertoire included many gospels and classics, but seldom an evening went by without his playing Floyd Cramer's "Last Date." (See https://www.youtube.com/watch?v=JvfG9uFswis.)

During the 1950s, Crader Equipment began selling chainsaws and lawnmowers to supplement company revenue. While International Harvester tractors were purchased directly from the factory, the saws and mowers were purchased from wholesale distributors. In 1959 a STIHL distributor located in nearby Illinois established Crader Equipment as a STIHL dealer.

Dad, then twenty-six years old, reached the conclusion that sales opportunities in a small, rural Missouri county were limited. He decided that becoming a wholesaler offered the greatest opportunity for growth. While investigating the wholesale distribution concept, he noticed a magazine ad soliciting STIHL distributors for Missouri. By then familiar with STIHL, he contacted the Tull-Williams company in New York to learn more about becoming a wholesale distributor. The Illinois distributor, who was focused on lawnmowers and garden tillers, consented to Crader Equipment assuming responsibility for STIHL in Missouri.

Buford and Don Crader trying Stihl's new Super Lightning

After an application and exchange of letters, Dad and Gordon Williams spoke on the phone. Soon thereafter, Crader Equipment placed an order for a chainsaw and was established as a STIHL dealer. Following rave reviews from local loggers, Dad convinced Buford—known to me as Papaw—to place an order for the minimum to become a distributor: forty chainsaws. This commitment required a bank loan—not a comfortable proposition for Papaw, who'd raised three children during the infamous Depression years, and like so many of his day, was averse to debt.

The nearest truck depot was thirty miles away, and a pallet of saws was too heavy to send UPS or USPS, so the first pallet of forty saws arrived by train. A spur of the Iron Mountain Railway ran through Marble Hill delivering general merchandise and fuel in, and carrying wood products and lead and iron ore out. The train depot was located less than a hundred yards from Crader Equipment. The train station was primarily a tie yard. There were several men familiar with timber cutting in general, and chainsaws in particular, working nearby. They were eager to join the Crader Equipment team and the entire Crader family when the doors to the boxcar were slid back revealing the neatly stacked pallet of new saws. It was the largest stack of new chainsaws anyone in the curious rural crowd had ever seen—a prescient moment. The saws were quickly loaded onto the Crader Equipment International Harvester flatbed pickup truck and later hidden in Papaw and Mamaw's (Leora's) basement. Papaw was sure it would take several years to sell them and pay off the loan.

Dad and Mom—by then both twenty-six years old and with two young children, and having partially paid down the home mortgage—returned to the bank for another loan: this time to purchase a used 1958 Chevrolet Impala with a Continental kit. Within a week Dad filled the trunk of the car with STIHL Lightnings and hit the road, calling on established chainsaw dealers from a list given to him by a lawnmower salesman. At first, most dealers weren't interested, but because of a good reference given to them by a trusted lawnmower salesman, a few offered to take a demo unit and get it into the hands of their chainsaw customers. Those who took demos usually ended up paying for the demo unit and selling it to a customer who'd formerly been using a Homelite or McCulloch. One by one, STIHL dealers were established, each ordering more saws, one at a time. As of this writing, a couple of those early dealers are still in business.

Having been a STIHL dealer before becoming a wholesale distributor, Dad understood the frequency of repair for chainsaws and the need for a quick and dependable source for replacement parts. Since the sales of units were still very slow, he had ample time to quickly ship replacement parts to the small but growing list of STIHL dealers. *Chain Saw Age* magazine eventually ran a story on Crader's parts service in which an order placed by 2:00 p.m. was generally shipped out the same day. It was the quality of the STIHL and the dependability of the parts service that endeared Dad and Crader Equipment to the growing number of STIHL dealers. Those two attributes remain at the top of the list for Crader Distributing and the STIHL dealers they serve today.

During the fall of 1961, Dad and Mom had their third child (a son) and purchased their first new car (a 1962 Chevrolet Impala), a carbon-copy duplicating machine, an AB Dick offset printing press, and a Grumman canoe. It was an eventful fall. The name they chose for their son was that of the person calling on them from STIHL at the time: Val.

Family vacations in those days consisted of drives through the heart of Missouri's hardwood region, where the oak for the staves that make the barrels holding world-renowned wine and whiskey are grown. Hardwood trees were among the most difficult to harvest for both man and machine—and remain so today. In those days nearly every small town in the hardwood region featured a chainsaw dealer, but only a few turned out to be reliable and creditworthy. The hardwood country is also home to numerous spring-fed, fast-running rivers, perfect for canoes.

Stan Musial at bat

Dad was a huge fan of Stan Musial, that's how I got my name. Fearful that 1962 might be Musial's final season as a player, Dad sprung for two tickets for Father's Day Sunday to watch the Cards and Giants. He and I got an early start for the long drive to Saint Louis to see Stan the Man. For Stan the boy, the chance to ride in the 327-cubic-inch, 4-barrel-carbureted '62 Chevy—by then with glass-packed dual exhaust—was almost as exciting as seeing Stan Musial and the Cardinals.

Stan the Man—at the age of forty-one and in the midst of one of his best years—was finishing the year second in the National League with an on-base percentage of .416 and was third in batting at .330. Being only six years old at the time, I didn't realize the significance of that particular game. Dad most likely used the fact that I had been named for Stan the Man as the reason to spring for the cost of the trip and the tickets to see one of his last games. The Cards throttled the Giants 13 to 3; Musial made four plate appearances, with two hits, one base on balls, and three runs batted in.

Years later, my wife, Debbie, and I would have the distinguished and rare honor of being invited to the home of Stan and Lillian Musial. Stan the Man and Lillian shared their story of being high school sweethearts at Pennsylvania's Donora High where Musial had played baseball with another budding star, Buddy Griffey, the grandfather of Ken Griffey, Jr.

Musial played for the St. Louis Cardinals from 1941 until 1963—except for 1945, when he was serving in the US Navy. During my visit with the Musials, I realized the enormity of the special day back in the spring of '62.

Baseball was an integral part of everyday life at the Craders. Teri, my older sister, and I spent nearly every summer Sunday afternoon and occasional weeknights watching Dad play town ball while we sold sodas from the back of the topless Scout. I still have the belt-mounted coin changer used while selling sodas from the Scout's tailgate, and the 33-1/3 RPM album of Harry Caray's radio broadcast from the 1964 World Series.

The carbon-copy duplicating machine, usually operated by Teri and me, was used for copying month-end statements Mom prepared and mailed to STIHL dealers. The offset machine—operated only by Dad, because it was both complicated and a mess to clean up—was used to mass produce homemade technical bulletins, price lists, sales promotions, and ad slicks for the dealers to use advertising STIHL. The Grumman canoe was used primarily for fishing but also for participating in canoe races on Missouri's famed Current River, which Dad discovered while prowling the Ozark hills for STIHL dealers.

Crader Equipment eventually became Crader Distributing Company, Inc. and hired their first salesman, devoted exclusively to calling on dealers who were selling STIHL and establishing new dealers. STIHL American rewarded Dad's commitment to STIHL and sales success by adding more territory to his responsibility, including the territory covered by the Illinois distributor who had established Crader Equipment as a STIHL dealer.

Dad—inspired by both a battery salesman who was a pilot and the flying STIHL distributor from Hood River, Oregon—earned his pilot's license and purchased a small Cessna for travel throughout the extended territory. One salesman eventually became two, and then there were three, and subsequently, more.

In 1974 Crader Distributing moved out of Crader Equipment into its own building, and for the first time, the wholesale operation had its own facility. Eventually, Dad and Mom moved out of their small nine-hundred-square-foot home and into a home with a real dining room, a living room large enough for a grand piano, and a fireplace to burn wood cut by a STIHL. By then they had a second daughter, Becki.

The once-small space in a damp basement devoted to warehousing a few STIHL saws grew to over two hundred thousand square feet of warehouse and an office dedicated exclusively to STIHL. The single saw that inspired the debt and risk necessary to purchase one pallet of saws in 1959 grew to over five hundred thousand units sold in 2015.

Dad found great pleasure in serving others. He was Marble Hill's first fire chief and, during his tenure, was instrumental in getting a tornado warning siren installed in the center of town. Soon after helping the town purchase its first new fire truck, he brought the shiny new truck to the school and demonstrated all the firefighting equipment for the students. I was a button-popping proud second-grader that day.

Dad was serving as Marble Hill's mayor when the city purchased land where a sod runway was built. Several local residents learned to fly using that airport, which was subsequently named for Ira Biffel, the man from near Marble Hill who taught Charles Lindbergh how to fly. To say dad was an adventurer is an understatement, as he flew over Cuba on his way from the Florida Keys to Mexico's Yucatan Peninsula, long before the days of GPS, and also hiked the Grand Canyon.

Dad would have given anyone the shirt off his back, but he didn't cater to those who tried to take what wasn't theirs. The only law enforcement in Marble Hill at the time was the county sheriff. Except in cases of emergency, people took care of themselves. After our warehouse had been broken into several times, we installed an alarm system. I was standing side by side with him one night after the alarm had sounded. We rushed to the warehouse in the topless Scout, where we encountered intruders. One of the intruders couldn't follow orders. A shooting occurred. Word got around. It was several years later before we had another break-in. One of my sons still has the infamous weapon that was used. It has several notches in the stock. I'll just leave it at that.

Dad enjoyed sharing his success with others. While he attended only one year of college, he believed a college degree to be important and wanted to help others by establishing scholarship endowments at Southeast Missouri State University, his alma mater, Hillsdale College in Michigan, and Truman State University in Missouri. Each year, over thirty students are able to attend college through assistance from one of Dad's endowments.

By 2014 the company that had begun as a small STIHL dealer, ordering one saw at a time, became a distributor with an order for forty—and eventually became STIHL's largest independently owned distributor. Dad's leap of faith resulted in a company with over two hundred thousand square feet of warehouse office space, selling over five hundred thousand powerheads per year, and supporting 150 families.

February 23, 2014, was a great day for Dad. After playing piano in church and enjoying lunch with friends, he came home and grabbed his STIHL blower. After clearing his driveway, he sat down on a garden-side bench. While admiring a job well done, he suffered a heart attack and slipped away. In the blink of an eye, he went from gazing on the green grass of home to being greeted at the gates of heaven. It was a lousy day for the rest of us but a glorious day for him.

While going through his personal affects, it was discovered that he'd made many personal loans to those who were pursuing a dream by starting a small business. Most loans had been paid back; some had taken decades to do so. I'm sure he considered each loan to be an investment in the community, and while he wished to be paid back, he didn't dwell on it if they weren't.

Thousands attended his funeral to pay respects and tell how he had personally impacted their lives. Some of those he'd helped financially tearfully shared their story at his visitation.

Pictured above is one of the last photos taken of Dad. He's proudly standing next to a STIHL tractor given to him by STIHL in recognition of his fiftieth year as a STIHL Distributor. The '62 Chevy, original duplicating machine, and offset printing press are long gone, but the Grumman is still hanging in his carport. The piano is sitting quiet in his living room. Some things are worth keeping.

It's emotionally moving to look back and realize that the touchdown of the KLM flight's return from Germany carrying the entire STIHL American team and the US distribution network marked the time when STIHL metaphorically took flight in America. The introduction of the fortieth-anniversary saw, the legendary 040, gave substantial lift to STIHL's already growing popularity among professionals, the primary chainsaw users at the time. A brand reaches a series of tipping points along the continuum of success. The introduction of the 040 was more of a launching point. The trip to Germany was well covered in trade publications confirming STIHL's commitment to the channel among dealers already handling STIHL, and aroused curiosity among dealers not convinced of the need to carry another brand of chainsaw, particularly one of foreign origin. It was the first of many trips.

Thereafter, distributor meetings designed to enhance relationships and foster the exchange of general business and marketing strategies became an annual event. Each January STIHL American distributors convened at a tropical destination, including Hawaii and the Caribbean. Five years later the group returned to Germany and Switzerland to witness the rapid expansion of STIHL's manufacturing capacity for saws, guide bars, and saw chain.

Chapter Twenty-One

THE COUNSELOR

BOB DYLAN WAS RIGHT: THE times, they were a-changin'. While publication of the STIHL Germany trip raised awareness of the brand among dealers, the 040 raised awareness among loggers. Soon, STIHL would be introduced to millions. Demand for the brand increased, and interest in selling and promoting the brand by enterprising people outside of the traditional power-equipment category occurred. Dorsey Glover, an Arkansas attorney, is a prime example.

On possibly the same day a Pan American Lockheed Super Constellation night flight from New York to Stuttgart, Germany, carrying Gordon Williams and Harding Smith on their quest to secure the famous one-page contract, a young, driven, and clever Dorsey Glover was sitting in an afternoon class on the sultry campus of the University of Arkansas. He was probably wishing he had drunk more coffee before attending class to suffer through a monotonous law professor droning on about torts. It's not likely that the lanky soon-to-be lawyer was sitting in class and obsessing about torts the way Gordon and Harding were obsessing about chainsaws, some eight thousand miles away. It would be nearly eight years before their paths would cross.

The only thing more deeply engrained into the DNA of a southern boy than respect for one's elders is pride. So, while one may follow the path of one's elders, it's important that doing so is the individual's decision. For Dorsey, the path of least resistance, or so he thought, was the pursuit of a law degree. A law degree, Dorsey claims, can be useful no matter one's vocation. He'd entered Arkansas's prestigious law school the previous semester so full of bluster that he didn't bother to begin attending classes until midterm, confident that it'd be a breeze, just as undergrad school had been. His New Year's surprise was a grade card full of Ds, a letter unfamiliar to him. It was a needed wake-up call to a gifted student for whom good grades had come easy. He realized law school was different, and so were the students. The classrooms were packed with eager, equally gifted, passionate students, serious about their education and future. The first-semester professors knew what they were doing and shocked Dorsey into a routine of long hours of study. The path of least resistance turned out to require hard work and focus, but once Dorsey assessed the landscape, he rose to meet the challenge.

The more sparsely populated the place of rearing, the more difficult it is for one to gain one's own identity. By the time a boy growing up in rural Arkansas reaches his teens, he's heard thousands of times, "Ain't you so-and-so's boy?" and "You gonna be a such-and-such just like your daddy when you grow up?" The more prominent one's lineage, the more likely this is to occur. Dorsey's grandfather was a two-term Arkansas state congressman, two-term US congressman, and a prominent local attorney. Dorsey's father was an equally successful attorney but better known for his entrepreneurial spirit. Dorsey had two large shadows from which to emerge.

Dorsey came of age in Malvern, Arkansas, the county seat of Hot Springs County, Arkansas, adjacent to a chain of lakes abundant with crystal clear water flowing from the Ouachita

Mountains, and near the well-known city of Hot Springs—which oddly enough, is not in Hot Springs County. Andy Griffith's Mayberry could very easily have been Malvern. Malvern and Mayberry shared many characteristics, which was the case for most small towns in America during the middle of the twentieth century: autonomous, everyone knowing everyone, the crooks few but known to all, and while citizens are sometimes hateful to each other, they're quick to defend even the staunchest opponent against outsiders. And just as in Mayberry, the sheriff in Malvern didn't carry a weapon.

There's a plethora of jokes circulating about Arkansans— such as why a toothbrush isn't called a teeth brush, and many more—but the peculiar fact is that most jokes about Arkansans are created by Arkansans. In Arkansas you either tell the joke or you're the feature of one.

Even though surrounded by heavily timbered forests and pulp mills, Malvern was better known as the brick capital of the world, according to Dorsey. In spite of being home to three Acme Brick plants—Weyerhaeuser, Georgia Pacific, International Paper— and other manufacturing facilities, during the 1950s Malvern's school district fell so miserably short of funds that the school year was shortened. Dorsey's parents—relatively affluent and wishing to make sure their son was the one telling the jokes and not the one about which the jokes were told, and in consideration of their fear of Russian mental superiority, soon thought to be confirmed with Sputnik—enrolled him in Columbia Military Academy, in Columbia, Tennessee. It was at Columbia that Dorsey began to emerge from the unspoken but ever-present grand paternal shroud. The future was his to choose, and he chose, albeit respectful of his father and grandfather, that which made the most sense for him. And somewhere along the line, he perfected the art of being the one telling the jokes.

Dorsey has always had and will likely always have mischief-suggesting, boyish facial features. During his experience at Columbia, he ceased being anybody's boy, and since he's much taller than average, it's obvious that he's not a boy. He sports a perpetual expression that can be a smirk, a smile, or a grimace, and no matter the circumstance, the expression doesn't change to any noticeable degree. I've observed Dorsey shaking hands and greeting those he admires and, on rare occasions, those he despises. The southern-bred courtesy gene necessitates Dorsey disguise his true feelings and make everyone feel special, even though in his mind he's conjuring up all sorts of humorous and undignified thoughts toward those whom he's looking down upon, both physically and virtually—albeit a rare occurrence. A careful observer realizes, at a glance, that Dorsey has a well-developed, clever, thoughtful, occasionally critical, but always humorous reply ready to spring forth. And based on the quip, tightly laced with fact, one can sense if he's sporting a smile or a smirk, most of the time.

To meet Dorsey is to appreciate the influence that his wife, Elaine, has had on him. She's a grand hostess, eager to entertain and share, and a superb conversationalist, versed on a wide variety of subjects. Dorsey occasionally gets a look from Elaine, and he realizes he's broken some arcane (in his mind) rule of etiquette. Elaine knew what she had bargained for when she met Dorsey—sometimes flashy, occasionally fancy, but always funny. Elaine is Dorsey's emotional anchor and compass. He still owns a '53 Ford Crown Victoria, the same color as the one in which he and Elaine had their first date while both were attending the University of Arkansas.

After graduating from the University of Arkansas School of Law, Dorsey easily passed the Arkansas Bar Exam and intended to return to Malvern, join his father's one-man law firm, and practice law until he figured out what he wanted to do, other than law. As a third-generation attorney, law was supposed to come natural, and it did, but he had an itch to do something more. Gaining a law degree was being true to his heritage, but being true to himself would take him beyond law.

In spite of following his own chosen path, his style and inclination differed little from that of his father, who while practicing law, also had holdings in two brick plants in Mississippi, two construction companies—one focused on bridges and highways and the other on buildings, hospitals, colleges, and large institutional structures. Dorsey's path was rich with opportunity. His father was essentially keeping the one-man practice open until Dorsey could take over. But the value of an opportunity depends on the enthusiasm and capacity of the one for which the opportunity is provided. Dorsey had heaping helpings of both, but his path would necessarily take a short detour.

On the day of graduation, Dorsey received a letter. Rather than return to Malvern immediately after graduation and having passed the bar, Dorsey respected an invitation from Uncle Sam and was inducted into the US Army Reserve as a second lieutenant. He completed basic training at Ft. Knox and then spent four months training with the Second Armored Division at Ft. Hood before returning home to Malvern and beginning to put to good use the many years of education. At last he opened his one-man law practice. Thanks to the Russians, he'd later be called upon once more to serve America.

Right away, he was asked to serve on the board of directors for the brick companies in which his father owned an interest, both located far away in Mississippi. Monthly trips to the brick plants were time consuming, so Dorsey purchased his first of several planes, a Cessna 210, shortening the travel time from eight hours of driving to two hours of flying. Since there wasn't an airport near either of the plants, Dorsey would set the plane down on a nearby dirt strip. Not only did the plane save them travel time, but it also allowed them the convenience of low flights over their competition's brickyards to check out their operations and inventory levels.

Dorsey assumed the role of lead counsel for the Bank of Malvern, the oldest state-chartered bank in Arkansas, and soon thereafter began serving on the board of directors.

As if practicing law and serving on the boards of multiple companies weren't enough, Dorsey began dabbling in real estate. One of his law practice clients—Robert Ward, of Ward Brothers Chainsaw Supply, a STIHL dealer/distributer and also pulp wood supplier for International Paper—was buying and selling timber and timberland. Dorsey and Robert became timber buying partners and the best of friends. They purchased timber to sell to International Paper and/or Georgia Pacific. In some cases they purchased the timber only and in other instances acquired the land, harvested the timber, and then sold or developed the land. Together they owned over twenty thousand acres of timberland at one time or another.

During a providential visit by Gordon Williams to Ward Brothers Chainsaw Supply, Robert introduced Dorsey and Gordon. Over dinner, Gordon shared his vision of STIHL in America. Dorsey's inherited entrepreneurial gene, and his favorable impression of Gordon and the vision of STIHL in America, combined to inspire him to strike a deal with Robert. Ward Brothers Chainsaw Supply had been selling for several years but primarily to sawmills, with which Robert was familiar. Gordon

Williams convinced Dorsey of the limitless opportunity of being a STIHL wholesale distributor.

While Ward Brothers Chainsaw Supply had been a good paying customer, they'd only been averaging about one saw per week, nearly the same as any good dealer at the time. Meanwhile, the two Missouri distributors to the north, Crader Equipment and Ozark Equipment—already covering the northern part of Arkansas—were ready and willing to take on the responsibility for the southern parts of Arkansas. "Not so fast," Dorsey likely thought. Representing sawmills other than Ward, Dorsey had heard many good reports about STIHL saws, and what he'd heard from Gordon confirmed those reports. Dorsey and Robert pooled their talents and resources and incorporated Ward Chain Saw Supply on April 1, 1966. Knowing Dorsey, I have to believe the date of incorporation, April Fool's Day, was not accidental.

Dorsey and partner, Robert Ward

Rainer, the whiz kid, always dreaded the Ozark Airline flight from Saint Louis to Malvern aboard a well-used DC-3 with its noisy, oil-slinging, vibrating, radial engines. Robert Ward's mechanic, with whom Rainer was familiar, always met him at the airport and drove him directly to Ward Brothers, only forty miles away. Rainer and Gordon had been concerned that Ward Brothers had not been experiencing sales increases equal to that of surrounding distributors, but Gordon was convinced that Dorsey would change that. Rainer's next trip was different from previous ones; rather than deal with technical issues, Rainer was to meet Robert's partner in the newly formed company.

Rainer and Dorsey met at a dinner hosted by Dorsey on the banks of Arkansas's Lake Catherine—where the vittles included fish that had been aged in the lake and liquid that had been aged in barrels, the staves of which had been made from Arkansas hardwood. Dorsey eyed Rainer suspiciously at first, but the combination of the aged drink and Rainer's innate charm turned the smirk into a southern smile, and the two became close friends.

The following day Rainer and Dorsey met at length in Dorsey's law office. Rainer shared what he knew about STIHL and the operations of other distributors. Dorsey told him of the decision to hire a salesman and "do it right." Rainer eventually moved to Malvern from California, a testimony to his impression of Dorsey and the Malvern area, and remained there until his return to Germany several years later.

Their first salesman, an ordained Baptist preacher, was from Hope, Arkansas, possibly Bill Clinton's childhood minister. Thankfully, he was good at selling saws. It was about that time that *Thunderball*, starring Sean Connery, and *Doctor Zhivago*, starring Omar Sharif, were in their first showings.

Andreas & Hannelore Stihl with Dorsey's father, son,
and ranch-hand.

Considering Dorsey's financial backing and visionary
addition to the Ward Brothers' established reputation and enterprise, Gordon offered Dorsey and Robert Ward the entire states of
Arkansas, Louisiana, and eventually, Texas.

During the early 1960s, Dorsey had made several flights
between Arkansas and the Dallas area. During those flights he
noticed that the dense timber forests of Arkansas and Louisiana
stopped about one county deep into Texas. And it was with that
knowledge that, when offered the entire state of Texas, he agreed
to taking responsibility for the thirteen easternmost counties in
Texas, those with abundant timber. He opted to let someone else
worry about the other 241 cacti- and rattlesnake-infested counties.
Dorsey now says that had he known then what he knows now,
he'd have taken the entire state of Texas and would now be "richer
than three feet up a bull's butt." But, as Dorsey says, "Hindsight
and bullshit are of equal value." Dorsey is full of quotable quotes
and sensible sayings, typical of Arkansans.

Peter Stihl and Dorsey next to Dorsey's Aero Commander.
Notice the number on the plane

After learning that a new distributor had been established in Arkansas, Don Crader (Dad) and I flew down to pay the new guy a visit. Dad, a recently licensed and inexperienced pilot, penetrated a rainstorm that turned out to be more than anticipated. Since the aerial map warned of rapidly rising terrain in the area, he had the good sense not to try and descend below the rain. We landed at the first airport we found after popping out on the back side of the storm, which turned out to be Arkadelphia, not far from our intended destination. After peeing our initials onto the chat ramp of the unattended airport and looking at a map, we made the short uneventful hop over to Malvern. Dad confirmed for Dorsey what he'd heard and learned about STIHL, Gordon Williams, and Rainer.

Dorsey sports a facial feature, other than the smirk, that is immediately noticeable. Everyone notices and nosey northerners ask. June 21, 1961, well before becoming Arkansas's two-time state skeet shooting champion, Dorsey had gained a reputation for owning guns and knowing how to use them. And it was on an otherwise normal afternoon in Malvern when he found himself with a trigger-pulling decision. While crossing Malvern's main street on the way from his office to the courthouse, he heard shots fired. He looked up the street and saw a man holding a rifle and shooting through the doorway of the local unemployment office. The shooter turned out to be a disgruntled man—well-known for being ornery, but not necessarily a killer, until then. He'd just shot and killed two and injured a third. Dorsey ran to his office and retrieved a .38 revolver. By the time he returned to the courthouse lawn, the shooter had run past a Chevy/Olds dealer and had shot a mechanic who'd innocently stepped outside to see what was going on. He then headed toward a junkyard, and while on the run, shot the spotlight off a Malvern police car.

The sheriff was unarmed but brave; the only weapon at his disposal was a machine gun with no clip, worth more as a display item in his office than as a weapon. He was literally outgunned. Knowing that Dorsey had guns, the sheriff sent Dorsey home to retrieve firearms as quickly as possible. Dorsey's car happened to be in the shop for repairs, so the sheriff loaned him a patrol car. Dorsey handed the sheriff the .38 revolver before racing home in the patrol car. Meanwhile, the sheriff and his deputies rushed into a nearby hardware store and requisitioned several rifles. By the time Dorsey returned with his weapons, including a legal 20-gauge double barrel pistol with 10-inch barrels, a Winchester 88 .308 caliber rifle, and another pistol, the shooter had escaped and hidden in a nearby junkyard.

Dorsey and a deputy slipped down an alleyway separating the junkyard from the backyards of a row of occupied homes. The sheriff headed to the entrance of the junkyard. By then, deputies from surrounding counties and several highway patrol officers were arriving on the scene. The shooter, seeing the large crowd moving in from the entrance, headed toward the alley, unbeknownst to Dorsey and the deputy. When the shooter spotted them, he took a shot. The bullet shattered when it struck a twelve-inch box elder tree. It was wide enough to shield Dorsey from the full impact of the round, but not wide enough to completely conceal his six-foot three-inch, 240-pound frame. While the thin tree likely saved Dorsey's life, a small fragment of the bullet struck his eye. Bleeding and with eye fragments on his suit sleeve, Dorsey moved out from the tree, drew down on the shooter, and gave him a choice: surrender or be shot. The shooter—still armed— chose wisely, moved cautiously in Dorsey's direction, and surrendered. A southern boy rarely steps fully from his father's shadow until well after the elder's funeral, but on that day Dorsey began casting a shadow of his own.

Dorsey could have easily and justifiably shot the killer on the spot, but he chose to let justice, his chosen profession at the time, take its due course. The killer was tried, found guilty, sentenced, and was provided three meals and a place to live at the taxpayers' expense for the rest of his life. Two other families in Malvern had to deal with the loss of a loved one for the rest of theirs. Dorsey learned to shoot with one eye—not as good as before, but better than most Texans with two.

Soon after Dorsey lost an eye to the rampaging murderer, the Russians decided to build a wall dividing Germany's communist-controlled sector from the free world. Their wall was very effective, by the way. Dorsey received notice from Uncle Sam that the United States needed more of him than serving in the reserve.

He was to report to Ft. Polk for active service duty in the US Army to join a medium duty tank outfit from his high school alma mater, Columbia, Tennessee. They were headed for Germany. Through a rare stroke of common sense, the US Army decided they could do better than an optically challenged lanky lawyer from Arkansas and granted him a full discharge on the same day that he was to report for duty at Ft. Polk.

Missing an eye may have been a condition making him ineligible to shoot artillery from a tank, but it clearly wasn't a handicap for shooting a .410 shotgun. Dorsey went on to be a two-time Arkansas state skeet shooting champion. As such, Dorsey received an invitation to participate in the San Antonio Gun Club's Inaugural National Skeet Shoot Tournament. The San Antonio Gun Club boasts of being the oldest gun club in America, and who's going to argue with a bunch of armed Texans? Inviting Dorsey from Arkansas assured the legitimacy of the national claim and the likely expectation was that nobody from Arkansas could shoot better than a Texan, at least not the best of Texas. It's a mystery that the San Antonio group thought so little of Dorsey since only a year earlier he'd posted the first ever perfect 100/100 with a .410 at the Dallas Gun Club. But that was way before online social platforms and the era of immediate sharing of all things, relevant or otherwise.

Texans believe the only good thing coming out of Arkansas is Interstate 30, so they didn't expect Dorsey to show up in San Antonio and win, but he did. In spite of showing up the Texans, Dorsey and Elaine were graciously hosted by STIHL's local distributor, Frank Gruen, and his wife, Ann. Frank was one of the few people who could virtually fill a room with presence, personality, and southern aura as quickly as Dorsey, and was equally blessed with a magnanimous wife. Perhaps Elaine and Ann quietly exchanged recipes for southern cuisine while Dorsey and Frank boisterously sipped expensive bourbon and talked STIHL and, of course, football. The Texas/Arkansas football rivalry had been going on since 1894. Most likely, Frank reminded Dorsey that Texas had the winning record in the football rivalry. Dorsey, having just bested the best of Texas, and being a gentleman, shared much with Frank, but not everything on his mind. Dorsey never tells all he knows, but you can always count on the fact that he's thinking of something.

For example, while drinking Frank's expensive bourbon, Dorsey didn't mention that he'd once been offered STIHL for all of Texas. And there was another thing Dorsey didn't mention, probably because it had yet to occur. He did remind Frank that he'd won the tournament with only one eye.

Dorsey and Robert Ward's partnership at Ward Brothers lasted until 1970 when Dorsey's vision of STIHL's potential exceeded that of Robert's. Robert's vision included owning Dorsey's three-hundred-acre farm. So, Robert and Dorsey struck a deal that resulted in Robert gaining a farm and some cash and Dorsey being the sole owner of Ward Saw Supply, renaming the enterprise STIHL Southwest. Soon thereafter, Dorsey built the first building designed exclusively for the distribution of STIHL saws, followed by the purchase of an IBM System 34, reportedly the first System 34 installed in the state of Arkansas. Like many of the early distributors, Dorsey was a successful one-of-a-kind, and not adverse to risk. The enterprise required considerable financial support. After several lean years, a dealer base was established, the STIHL line of products expanded, and STIHL Southwest became profitable, selling STIHL exclusively.

*Fred Whyte pointing out Dorsey's superior market
penetration numbers*

Nearly the entire Stihl family took the time to visit Dorsey and
Elaine at least once, an event few distributors can boast. During
one such visit, Dorsey had the chance to share with Andreas the
results of a local chainsaw-cutting competition. Dorsey's new
salesman had expressed some concern at competing with a brand
known for running at a very high RPM and being very loud.
Dorsey told the salesman that RPMs and noise didn't cut logs:
power did. With that, the salesman confidently competed and
won.

Oh, the thing Dorsey didn't tell Frank while drinking his
liquor . . . glad you asked. While Arkansas rarely beat Texas in

football, STIHL Southwest, when compared to all other US distributors, ranked first or second every year in market penetration, a feat Frank's company never came close to matching. Some could argue that Dorsey had the advantage, with Rainer the whiz kid choosing Malvern as his home in America, followed up by the budding all-star Fred Whyte as his STIHL representative, and also choosing Arkansas as his home base. Those were both advantages; however, STIHL Southwest's stellar numbers and market penetration success continued long after the departure of both Rainer and Fred to elevated positions within the STIHL organization. And for that matter, the excellent market performance continues well into Dorsey's semiretirement days. Dorsey ranks high on the metrics that matter most: moral, spiritual, financial, and being an excellent, patient mentor. He honored and followed the path his father and grandfather made, as far as it went, and then extended it with footprints of his own.

Power equipment dealers have many choices; those in the south chose Dorsey and continue to choose STIHL Southwest.

Chapter Twenty-Two

TOSSING SAWS IN KANSAS

STIHL's POPULARITY EVENTUALLY REACHED THE windswept high plains of Kansas. A Wichita-based tree service first became interested in STIHL for personal purposes. They soon realized the profit potential of selling saws rather than purchasing them to use.

Glenn Banks was born November 25, 1902, in Columbus, Ohio, to Lewis Banks, a railroad conductor, and Barbara Calhoun Banks, reportedly a relative of the late John C. Calhoun, who was famous for serving as vice president for both John Quincy Adams and Andrew Jackson.

Glenn earned a degree in Forestry Management in Mansfield, Ohio, near where the legendary Johnny Appleseed allegedly planted the first of his many apple trees. Immediately following graduation, Glenn accepted a position with the city of Saint Louis managing the trees in the city's many beautiful parks—including the famed Forest Park, known then and now as one of the great urban parks of America.

While attending college he fell for the charms of a Mansfield girl, Henrietta Freese. Henrietta waited until Glenn's job with the city was secure and he'd proven himself to be a dependable provider before accepting his marriage proposal. They were married November 1927 and settled in an apartment with a view of Forest Park, only a few blocks from St. Mary's hospital, where Henrietta gave birth to their son, Jack Banks, July 1930.

Doors seem to open for those with extraordinary skills and ethics and especially for those willing to make commitments and follow the opportunity. Through the arborist network, Kansas Gas and Electric (KG&E) learned of the job that Glenn was doing in Saint Louis. KG&E, in the process of establishing electric service in and around the Wichita area, needed rights-of-way cleared so electric lines could be run to provide electric service throughout Wichita and surrounding communities. Glenn eagerly responded to the call and, sensing opportunity, headed west.

Although he was born in Denison, Texas, Dwight Eisenhower was only two when his parents moved to Kansas, where they raised him. Dwight disappointed his pacifist parents by attending West Point, but then made them proud by commanding the US Forces in Europe and, eventually, being elected president of the United States. He created the interstate highway system, tailored after Germany's famed autobahn. Many today think that communities have been established along the interstate system. In fact, the reverse is true; the highway system was created to join established communities and facilitate the efficient flow of goods north, south, east, and west.

The first interstate highway—a short segment of I-70—was completed in 1956, west of Topeka, Kansas, near Eisenhower's boyhood home, Abilene. By 1970 a 424-mile segment of I-70 stretched across the entire state of Kansas, the longest contiguous interstate corridor at the time.

While driving west on I-70, one will notice a significant drop in population density and a gradual geological transformation once having crossed the north/south I-35 artery. Annual rainfall west of I-35 drops off precipitously and there's visual evidence along the entire I-35 corridor. I-35 connects cities that were the last stop before continuing west. Even today, few cities of any size exist between I-35 and I-25, except in the petroleum fields.

Wichita, situated on I-35 and the Arkansas River, is one of those great legendary towns that made up what was once known as the western frontier. It was the last source of supplies before heading for California. Wichita is as far west as Glenn and Henrietta moved before, like the tallgrass of the prairie, they established deep, lasting, and permanent roots.

Under new leadership, KG&E decided to outsource the right-of-way maintenance and clearing. Rather than see the outsourcing as an elimination of his job, Glenn made lemonade out of lemons, formed Banks Tree Service, and earned KG&E's business. While KG&E expanded rapidly into surrounding communities and counties, Banks Tree Service, devoted and committed to KG&E, added crews and equipment accordingly.

Glenn's son, Jack E., and Mariann Asmann met while attending Wichita's East High School. They were married in 1951, just prior to Jack's two-year US Army deployment to Japan. Upon his return from Japan, Jack joined Glenn in the business and attended Wichita University, where he earned a liberal arts degree in business. Jack and Glenn were a team: one with a business degree and the other forestry.

In a business decision designed to reduce their cost of equipment, Jack and Glenn purchased a small white building on Wichita's East Central Street. They established a budding equipment business—aptly named Central Equipment—where they sold many of the items they used at Banks Tree Service. Doing so reduced their cost of equipment at Banks Tree while retail sales of the equipment augmented their profit, which they used to diversify by investing in real-estate and rental property. Eventually, through hard work and smart management, they had two businesses: retail sales of chainsaws, lawn mowers, kerosene heaters, log splitters, go-karts; and the core business, Banks Tree Service.

In the same way as word had gotten to KG&E about Glenn, word had gotten to STIHL American about the volume of Homelites being sold by Central Equipment. It was early 1967 when Rainer Gloeckle called on Glenn and Jack. After a brief introduction, Jack asked Bill Hildebrandt, the foreman of his tree service—a quintessential lumberjack of a man, large and knowledgeable about saws—to join them. Hildebrandt, sporting a German name, a no-nonsense demeanor, and devoted to Homelite, was willing to listen. Jack's young son, Stan, looked on.

Stan Banks recalls Rainer first getting the attention of all by tossing a running STIHL 08 across the parking lot and then leaving it lying upside down and still idling. While the saw continued to idle, Rainer, using another saw, demonstrated the ease with which a STIHL 08 could be dismantled and, while doing so, showed them the precision fit of the parts. Rainer then pulled out a velvet Seagram's bag containing a cylinder and ring-free piston and demonstrated the close tolerances of the Mahle chrome-impregnated piston and cylinder. Actions always speak louder than words.

Glenn, getting along in years and knowing he'd be retiring soon, gave the decision-making to Jack. Jack—being a bit of a skeptic, for which Kansans are well-known—needed a few days to consider putting STIHLs on his tree service trucks. An avid and accomplished bowler, Jack spent a few nights at the lanes contemplating the opportunity. With the endorsement of Bill Hildebrandt, Jack and Glenn decided to give STIHL a try by equipping several of their crews with STIHLs.

Soon afterward, Rainer convinced Jack to become the first STIHL distributor for Kansas and Nebraska, but the opportunity came with another difficult decision—selling Banks Tree Service and devoting all their attention to STIHL. This was a much bigger decision and would require selling a company with over seventy employees, an enterprise that represented Glenn's lifetime achievement. Jack and Glenn, both Freemasons, likely consulted their fellow Masons about their decision.

Only a few months after equipping several of their Banks Tree Service trucks with STIHL and learning more about STIHL Germany and STIHL American, they sensed the opportunity to get in on the ground floor of a promising enterprise. Jack and Glenn, with the consent of Henrietta and Mariann, made the decision to divest themselves of all other business interests and commit to STIHL. The new business kept the name, Central Equipment, as a way to secure the legacy of what was started in the little white building on Wichita's East Central Street. A new adventure was given birth. The Kansans proved to be up to the task.

I-35 divides Kansas, running from the Oklahoma border, just south of Wichita, north to Kansas City—leaving about 90 percent of Central Equipment's Kansas and Nebraska territory west of the line. Leaning on the reputation of Banks Tree Service, known throughout Kansas and Nebraska for being reliable and trustworthy, Jack hit the road convincing Homelite and McCulloch dealers to give STIHL a try. Since Jack was the former owner of a renowned arborist's service, opening doors was made easier, but that didn't make sales automatic.

Unlike the forests east of I-35, which are regularly harvested for lumber, the forests west of I-35 are coveted, and parks have been established in the few places where trees are plentiful.

Kansas is known for its Flint Hills, Nebraska for Chimney Rock, and both states for the ruts in the prairie desert floor made by wagons crossing along the famed Oregon Trail; neither state is known for trees.

Like many others at the time, Jack left home on Monday and returned on Friday, leaving Mariann at home with their two children, Stan and Danna. At the time, Central Equipment was one of the largest STIHL distributors geographically but it had the fewest trees and people. The distance between towns was great, and the widely dispersed towns were sparsely populated. The lack of trees didn't quench Jack's entrepreneurial spirit. "Trees don't buy saws; people buy saws," he was known to have said while sporting a confident grin.

With each new dealer came an order for a few saws, and with each saw sold at retail came parts sales, and eventually guide bars and saw chain, followed by other chainsaw accessories. As Central Equipment grew so did the staff, one employee at a time. STIHL slowly and methodically expanded the chainsaw line and eventually introduced new categories of products, namely lawn care tools.

STIHL is unique in many advantageous ways. One of the features is family. While STIHL has grown to be the number-one-selling brand of outdoor handheld power tools, the company is still family owned and operated. And all of STIHL's independent distributors are family owned and operated. Family members generally don't join the business; they grow up in the business, which was the case with Jack and Mariann's son, Stan.

Stan was able to observe Rainer Gloeckle's saw-tossing demonstration because at the age of twelve, he was at Central doing janitorial chores. After working his way through several positions, including receiving, shipping, technical services, and customer service, Stan hit the road calling on dealers throughout Central's vast Kansas and Nebraska territory. Meanwhile, Jack hired a new office assistant. Lori caught Stan's eye, and even with knowledge of the business and of the commitment on Stan's part to serve Central's dealers, the two became a couple and eventually married, adding another husband and wife team at Central Equipment.

By the time Jack reached retirement age, he recognized that in order for a distributor to provide all the necessary services for dealers and help them operate efficiently so they could profitably compete, it would be better if STIHL distributors merged, thus creating greater efficiencies of scale for themselves and expanding their services to the STIHL dealer. To this end Jack approached a bordering distributor (Crader Distributing) with the idea of merging. The concept was successfully presented to STIHL. Crader and Central Equipment merged in what was the first of many mergers between STIHL distributors, resulting in Jack's vision of greater economies of scale for the distributor and expanded services to the dealer. Today there are ten STIHL distributors where there were once nearly fifty. STIHL is the number-one selling brand of outdoor power tool in America, and the market share in Kansas and Nebraska leads the country.

While no longer selling STIHL, the Banks spirit of commitment continues. Stan and Lori gave birth to Alaina and Jeremy. Jeremy is now serving in the United States Marine Corps. A greater commitment doesn't exist.

Chapter Twenty-Three

A STIHL FIRST

SINCE JOINING STIHL AMERICAN, FRED Oswald had been persistently petitioning for STIHL to pursue the consumer market by placing an ad in *Life Magazine*. With the help of Gordon's cousin, Fred finally got his way—a first for STIHL.

Life Magazine was arguably the greatest magazine at the time. It featured giant full-color photos when few people had cameras, and a good photograph was a rare commodity. *Life* was highly acclaimed and anxiously anticipated by families all across America, especially during the war years. One of the most famous postwar photos ever taken was of a sailor kissing a nurse during the ticker tape parade in New York City. Starting in April 1952, Marilyn Monroe graced the front cover several times, including the issue following her mysterious death. If a picture is worth a thousand words, then each *Life* publication was worth millions.

At the 1936 launch of *Life Magazine*, Henry Luce, founding editor, pithily explained the magazine's intended purpose: "To see life, to see the world, to watch the faces of the poor, and the gestures of the proud, to see strange things, machines, armies, multitudes, and shadows in the jungle, to see, and to take pleasure in seeing, to see and be instructed, to see and be amazed." Luce continued with the magazine's business strategy: "Business, more than any other occupation, is a continual dealing with the future; it is a continual calculation, an instinctive exercise in foresight."

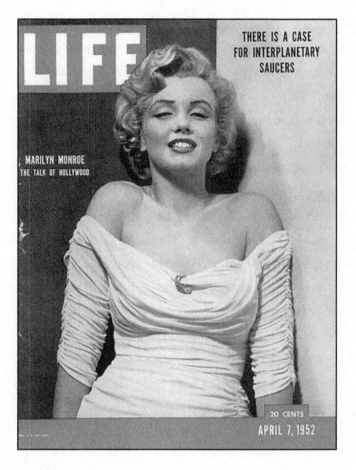

Much of STIHL's success is due to an instinctive exercise in foresight on the part of all channel members, including end users who are willing to pay more for a tool that will last long into that aforementioned future. Until October 7, 1966, no chainsaw company had ever placed a full-page ad in the coveted, well read, widely circulated, and expensive *Life Magazine*. Fred Oswald and director of advertising for *Life*, Malcolm Scott—married to Gordon's first cousin—convinced Gordon to make the unprecedented investment. The placement of the full-page ad, costing more than 50 percent of STIHL American's net worth at the time, turned out to be a wise move—foresight, risk, initiative.

Gordon targeted the October 7, 1966, issue for a special reason: his mother's birthday. She'd passed away a year earlier, but Gordon honored her nonetheless. His father had abandoned the family when Gordon was nine. Throughout the depths of the Great Depression, in order to save a nickel, she'd walk three miles to the Paterson school where she taught.

The STIHL 040 had introduced a new generation of chainsaws to the world. The full-page *Life Magazine* ad, with the 040 as the subject, introduced the STIHL brand and STIHL's support for independent dealers to millions of American families. Note the text that informs readers that STIHL saws are available only at authorized servicing dealers. The massive hands and forearms holding the saw are those of Man of STIHL, Ernie Rainey. This marketing investment was made when other brands, more dominant than STIHL at the time, were abandoning their dealer commitments. The risky investment and pioneering strategy paid handsome dividends for all members of the STIHL channel.

Chapter Twenty-Four
THE TIDE TURNS

STIHL'S MARKET SHARE GAINS CAUSED competitive brands to make decisions that reaped extraordinary short-term gains but proved fatal in the long term. Homelite made their product available to Sears, and McCulloch applied pressure on their distributors to rapidly and significantly increase their dealer count. One of McCulloch's largest customers, Bud Bryan, refused to compromise his principles and dropped the line, even though it was his primary source of income. McCulloch's decision would eventually lead to their failure; Bryan's decision would ultimately lead to unparalleled success.

News of Bryan Equipment's shocking decision traveled fast. Jimmy Hampton, familiar with the Bryan organization and the representative calling on STIHL American for Omark, the world's largest saw chain manufacturer at the time, made sure that Gordon and Ernie heard the latest news regarding McCulloch's prize distributor.

Genealogy is always tedious and rarely interesting, especially when it deals with an unrelated family. We now know that genetics play a significant role in our health and behavior. It's easy to recognize the effects of genetics in animals—retrievers naturally retrieve, beagles chase rabbits, and Chihuahuas bark. The same natural tendencies occur in humans.

The Bryans have traced their genealogy all the way back to Sir

Francis Bryan, who served as governor general of Ireland in 1549. The following reads like something out of the book of Numbers in the *Bible*, but it is representative of the journey of many American families.

Francis was the father of William, who was the father of Morgan, who immigrated to Virginia and married Martha Stroode, an orphan. Morgan and Martha had nine children including a son, William. William married Mary Boone, sister of famed explorer, Daniel Boone. William and Mary moved to North Carolina where they had ten children. Samuel, the oldest son, married Mary Hunt in 1775 and moved to Kentucky. Samuel and Mary had eleven children, including a son, Luke. Luke married Mary Sanders in 1807, and together they had twelve children, including a son, John Samuel. John married Harriet Hartman in 1854. John and Harriett had six children including a son, Homer. Homer married Rachel Friend in 1879. Homer and Rachel had two sons including Frederick. Frederick married Gertie Kahn in 1906, and to them was born Frederick II in 1912 in Saint Joe, Missouri.

Since he was the second Frederick, he was nicknamed Bud, which he preferred to Junior. Bud, following the footsteps of his father, attended the University of Indiana (IU), where he excelled in football and track. During the summer months, he worked as a lifeguard at the Grand Hotel on Mackinaw Island, Michigan—not a bad gig for a college kid. His scholastic achievements at IU paled in comparison to later accomplishments.

After graduation from IU, Bud made two decisions that would set the course of his life. He proposed to Kay Parr. Kay was a formidable lady born in Amarillo, Texas, in 1913, into a family renowned for large construction projects—the most well-known being the historic Santa Fe, New Mexico, train station. Although

Kay's father was no fool and not impressed with Bud's ancestry—including an Irish governor and the sister of Daniel Boone—the wedding would receive his blessing and occur only after Bud got a job.

Bud gained employment with a highly respected Chicago firm, the Arthur Mall Tool Company, selling—among other things—STIHL chainsaws. Bud and Kay were married in 1935. With the job, Bud had a wife and a STIHL; both would serve him well.

In 1940, Frederick Bryan III (Rick) was born to Bud and Kay.

In 1941, the United States banned the import of German products and ceased patent protection for German manufacturers. Mall Tool, no longer able to get STIHLs, began to manufacture their own saw, copied after STIHL's patented design, and went to market with a saw bearing his name, a chainsaw commonly referred to as a Mall.

In 1944, the job at Mall Tool took the family to Cincinnati, where the Bryan family remains to this day.

Meanwhile, Bob McCulloch, born in Saint Louis in 1910, was the son of an industrialist who'd made a fortune building Thomas Edison electrical power plants. Bob's wife, Barbara, was the daughter of Stephen Briggs, of Briggs and Stratton fame. After watching the growth of the chainsaw market, Bob used his financial wherewithal and the in-law familial small engine connection to start a small engine manufacturing company—McCulloch Motors Company. When McCulloch decided to manufacture chainsaws, he looked for those who'd been the most successful at selling saws. He offered them a deal they couldn't refuse. Rather than hire salesmen to sell his product, he offered those who'd proven to be leading salesmen in the chainsaw category a distributorship—a chance to own their own company, take their own risks, and reap the results of their efforts.

In 1948, Bud Bryan got the call. Bryan Equipment was formed and moved into the company's first location: Bud and Kay's basement. Bud hit the road selling McCullochs, and Kay handled the shipments.

In 1950, Bryan Equipment's 2.5-person (the .5 was eight-year-old Frederick III—Rick) operation moved into a two-story building with offices upstairs and shipping operations in the basement. Bud, using what he'd learned while working for Arthur Mall, grew the business one dealer at a time by providing a quality product and excellent customer service.

In spite of being a competitor of Mall Tool Company, Bud remained respectful of Arthur Mall and Mall Tool Company. Rick III tells a story of when he was only ten years old and helping man a Bryan Equipment booth at the Indiana State Fair. He took some McCulloch brochures and handed them out while standing in front of the Mall Tool booth. For that, he was rewarded with a highly effective and painful consequence of disrespect. Unfortunately, it's a lesson rarely taught today.

In 1954, Bryan Equipment moved into its third location, which they shared with Hoobler Printing for ten years. Roger Staubach, of Dallas Cowboys' fame—who married one of the Hoobler girls and, like Rick III, played football—attended a rival high school against which Rick's school played a practice game. Rick has conveniently forgotten the score of the game.

By 1965, Bryan had grown to be McCulloch's second-largest distributor—covering Ohio, Indiana, and Kentucky. The company moved to a location of their own—no more sharing parking lots, utility bills, and having the temporary, uncertain sense that prevails in a shared environment. It was a move that positioned them for greater things to come.

The company experienced their first major tragedy when the salesman covering Eastern Kentucky died of a massive heart attack. He was alone in a hotel room in Mt. Sterling, Kentucky, and left behind a wife and three children. With the bad comes the good: Frederick II (Bud) asked Frederick III (Rick) to join the company.

After attending the University of Cincinnati—much to the chagrin of his father and grandfather, who'd attended Indiana University—and following a stint serving the United States in the US Army, Rick joined ARMCO Steel, where he performed so well he was promoted ahead of other, more experienced veteran salespeople. One of the perks he'd earned along with the promotion at ARMCO was a company car with air conditioning: a 1964 Ford Falcon four-door station wagon. Upon Bud's offer to join the family business, Bryan Equipment purchased the car, leaving Rick with the need to explain to veteran salesmen how the owner's son's company car was the only company car with A/C.

The sixties were a time of significant change in retail America. Small independent shops that had served rural America for decades began to lose market share to nationally branded outlets. Sears, originally a mail-order watch shop in 1886, had grown to be the largest retailer in the country with locations in nearly every urban setting in America. At that time, Sears was selling a wide variety of items including prefabricated houses, items for the house, insurance for home and auto, and much more, including clothing and sports equipment. The list could fill a catalog, which it did.

JC Penney, another Missouri boy, had grown his retail organization from a small store in Wyoming in 1902 to one of Sears's major competitors. In 1940, JC Penney hired a young fellow by the name of Sam Walton. Walton would eventually leave JC Penney and build a retail empire that would eclipse Sears and JCPenney combined. The popularity of these one-stop shopping outlets, with lower prices as a result of their enormous buying power and their nationally branded marketing campaigns, began to make it more difficult for the small independent outlets to compete.

Homelite introduced the XL12, kicking off a tumultuous era in the chainsaw industry. Up until that time, dealers across the United States typically chose to sell either Homelite or McCulloch, and many small towns had two dealers—one selling Homelite and the other McCulloch with one or the other selling a few STIHLs. Homelite's introduction of the XL12 tilted the market share balance so dramatically that McCulloch began demanding their distributors set up more dealers and, in many instances, insisting they do so regardless of the market potential. As mentioned, one of McCulloch's largest distributors, Bryan Equipment, valued their dealer loyalty more than that of their relationship with McCulloch.

Homelite was likely the first major chainsaw manufacturer to break from the traditional wholesale channel strategy and begin selling directly to a major retail chain: Sears. This move befuddled the traditional independent full-service dealer who had been instrumental in establishing Homelite as a major brand in the chainsaw category. McCulloch, having slightly more respect for the traditional channel but sensing the need to accommodate the conglomerates, approached their distributors with a different but equally disruptive proposition—more dealers at any cost.

In 1966, McCulloch called a special meeting at which they asked (demanded) all distributors to begin selling to JCPenney TBA stores. TBA stores were JCPenney stores with tires, batteries, and an accessory department. JCPenney TBA stores were already selling and servicing a variety of products that used small engines, so McCulloch's request wasn't ludicrous, but as with Homelite, it is likely the point in time that marked the beginning of the end for both well-known and, up until then, highly respected companies.

For Bud, the violation of his principles by McCulloch was clear, but the ramification of losing McCulloch was heavy on his conscience. He'd built the business by establishing dealers based on the local market need and the ability of the dealer to appropriately service the product sold — one dealer at a time. Bud's decision to refuse to comply with McCulloch's request would cost him the distributorship. Based on principle it was an easy decision, but that didn't make the decision simple; it was complicated. Based on fiduciary responsibility — considering that Bud now employed the primary provider for over twenty families, including his son, and had just moved into what was then a state-of-the-art facility — declining McCulloch's mandate was potentially disastrous for his family and his loyal employees.

Poulan, a well-known saw manufacturer at the time, jumped at the chance to convert McCulloch's largest distributor to Poulan. Bud Bryan rewarded Poulan with a record-setting order once Poulan agreed to grant Bryan exclusive distribution over the same area they'd covered for McCulloch.

It was then that Jimmy Hampton notified Gordon Williams of McCulloch's faux paus and that Bryan was in the final stages of taking on Poulan. Ernie Rainey was on the next plane to Cincinnati.

Providentially, just prior to being contacted by STIHL American, Bud Bryan received word from Poulan that Bryan Equipment would not be allowed to sell Poulan throughout their entire established territory. Bud had, only days earlier, been fretting about the fiduciary predicament that had been the result of standing on principle, and now he was faced with another momentous decision. He called a special meeting of his sales staff and asked their advice. While they were disappointed to not have Poulan, a better-known brand at the time, they recalled dealers having spoken about STIHL, and a few dealers already selling STIHL and getting very good reviews. Based on the salesmen's input and sensing an opportunity, Bud terminated the arrangement with Poulan. It's possible that Bryan Equipment holds the record for being a Poulan distributor for the shortest length of time.

With details between STIHL American and Bryan Equipment worked out, and an agreement consummated with a handshake, Bud Bryan placed an order with STIHL American that was the largest order they'd ever received and represented more saws than STIHL American had sold in the entire country the previous year. Bryan Equipment, with one order, became STIHL's largest distributor and remained so for several decades. In a single day, Bryan Equipment went from being relatively unknown to the Stihl family in Germany to one of their largest customers.

To everyone's delight, dealers enthusiastically changed their orders from Poulans to STIHLs. It's likely the full-page *Life Magazine* ad had something to do with many dealers having already received calls about STIHL and recognizing the name.

Working out the details of how Bryan Equipment would be able to represent STIHL throughout their already established dealer network required STIHL American to negotiate buyout deals or termination agreements with the several small distribu-tors already established in the proposed Bryan coverage area. One of the distributors that had to be dealt with was United Welding Company of Wellington, Ohio—the very first STIHL distributor in America, established during the Tull-Williams era. An amicable agreement was reached, and United became one of Bryan's first dealers.

A deal was struck with Ken Hueber, owner of Farm & Forest, the Cincinnati-based STIHL distributor at the time. Ken became STIHL American's regional manager, whose only account was Bryan Equipment. Since the deal relieved Ken of the pressures of ownership and likely increased his annual income, he eagerly agreed to the terms. He became an extraordinary asset to the STIHL American organization and eventually went on to perform paralegal services and remained with STIHL until retirement.

Rapp's Repair of Beaver, Ohio—possibly the oldest STIHL dealer in America—was among the dealers Bryan inherited in the massive restructuring of Ohio, Indiana, and Kentucky. Rapp is still in operation at the time of this writing.

Rick continued to represent Bryan Equipment and STIHL on the road for a few more years before joining management and being mentored for an executive position. He recalls numerous stories about life as a STIHL salesman during the early years. His stories are similar and representative of those told by others.

Possibly the most remarkable and telling story of the commitment by STIHL American to STIHL and their distributors is one by Ernie Rainey, VP of sales and marketing for STIHL American. The 1967 Paul Bunyan show, a mainstay for those selling chainsaws, was held in Mansfield, Ohio. The nearest airport served by commercial airlines was in Columbus. After arriving in Columbus, Ernie learned there were no rental cars available, so he simply started walking and hitchhiking to the show, seventy miles away. This type of effort, while extraordinary, wasn't unique.

STIHL road warriors, those responsible for managing a territory and finding and establishing dealers, occasionally must cancel dealers. Rick had one such case in an area in which it was common for dealers to carry sidearms. When the local dealer no longer met his obligations, Rick cancelled the dealer by phone rather than take the risk of doing so in person—particularly in consideration of the fact that said dealer had a questionable reputation, a General Patton demeanor, and the habit of wearing a large-caliber, pearl-handled, well-used revolver. In this particular county, the sheriff had once hauled Rick to the sheriff's office under the guise of arrest, only to ask for a demo saw.

Years later the area was being handled by Rick's replacement, Bill Lucas. Times had changed, and Bill found the need to cancel the dealer that Rick had set up and reestablish the dealer that Rick had cancelled. When Bill returned to the former dealer, who was still sporting the pearl-handled weapon, and offered him the dealership, he was told by the dealer that the prior gutless wonder had cancelled him, and he would never handle STIHL again. Bill simply told the dealer that Rick had been fired long ago, at which time the dealer agreed to resume carrying STIHL.

Rick once followed an empty logging truck to see where it was getting logs. The trip took him deep into the Appalachian back country to a remote logging camp. The crews were harvesting Tulip Poplars, the same species as the legendary Revolutionary War-era Liberty Trees. In this instance they were being harvested for North Carolina furniture companies. There wasn't a STIHL to be found. Rick found the foreman and convinced him to demo a STIHL 07 and 090. After the demo, the loggers were agreeable to trying STIHL but insisted that Rick stay for dinner. The dining hall was rugged but clean. The table was set, and each setting had a small water glass, which turned out to be a large shot glass. Following a robust dinner, the cook poured everyone several ounces of 150-proof moonshine. Rather than risk life or limb by refusing to drink the hillbilly kerosene, Rick downed it. A few macho-preserving shots later—and after getting an order for several saws, which were later delivered to the local dealer— Rick staggered to his car and headed to the nearest hotel, which was hours away.

Bud continued to lead the company for several years before handing operations over to Rick in 1974, who gave the reins to Tom Jones in 1991. Tom mentored and then handed the company over to Frederick IV (Rick IV) in 2008. Bryan Equipment, a company that exudes high ethics, continues to set the example in wholesale distribution and now serves over 1,500 STIHL dealers throughout Michigan, Ohio, Indiana, Kentucky, Tennessee, and West Virginia from an impressive and state-of-the-art 125,000 square-foot facility.

Bryan Equipment, following Bud Bryan's series of calculated decisions and principled example, is now in the company's third generation. Having defied statistical odds of survivorship for family-owned businesses, it now sells over five hundred thousand STIHL units each year, and has become the envy of the power equipment industry.

Chapter Twenty-Five
HE COULD HAVE GONE PRO

HIS FATHER WAS EMPLOYED WITH the civil service at Wright-Paterson Air Base. He grew up just down the street a few blocks from the garage where the Wright Brothers designed the first airplane. One would assume that during his formative years he'd dreamed of strapping on a leather helmet, wrapping his neck with a silk scarf, becoming an airborne swashbuckler, and barnstorming across America. Rather than using a vacant field to fly kites or balsam model airplanes and idolize Ohio's Eddie Rickenbacker, Jimmy Hampton migrated to the field where America's favorite sport was being played—baseball. His idol was a different Ohio hero, Cy Young. Jimmy's dream was pitching in the majors. Like very few, he almost made it, but like most, he didn't.

Baseball took him to Miami of Ohio, where he met his wife. STIHL took him to New Hampshire, where he and Barb raised a family. After living there for over fifty years, he and Barb call the White Mountains of New Hampshire home. They can see the tallest peak of the Presidential Range, Mt. Washington, from their kitchen window.

He was born and raised in Dayton, Ohio. During the1940s, his family moved temporarily to lower Alabama, near Mobile. It was there—at age twelve, while participating in a baseball clinic—that baseball's legendary Eddy Stanky recognized Jimmy's extraordinary left-handed pitching ability and told him to check back when he turned seventeen. Stanky's encouragement boosted Jimmy's passion for the majors and the notion that his dream might become reality.

When reflecting on missed opportunities, Jimmy harks back and regrets having not made contact with Eddy. It would have been so easy since, after reaching the age of accountability, he came within baseball spitting distance of Stanky while attending a Cincinnati Reds and St. Louis Cardinal's game. He and a buddy had field-side seats, compliments of a friend of Reds' outfielder, Guss Bell. When asked why he didn't say something to Stanky, Jimmy shrugs and recalls being momentarily without the ability to breathe or think after speaking to and getting an autograph from the great Stan Musial. It's possible that out of respect for Guss, who'd treated them to the game, that Jimmy didn't reach out to Stanky, just a few feet away in the Cards' dugout. Jimmy's eyes take on a distant look, he shrugs, lets go a chuckle, and says, "It wasn't meant to be."

Jimmy admiring his billboard

Even though he came of age in the state known as the birthplace for aviation, Jimmy was never interested in flying. He recalls attending school primarily to play baseball. Looking back, he says baseball was the most important thing in his life during the formative years. Stanky's observation was confirmed when the Detroit Tigers offered Jimmy a minor league contract, which included college courses at the University of Wisconsin. After visiting Wisconsin, Jimmy decided to stay in Ohio and take advantage of a baseball scholarship offer by Miami of Ohio. His primary reason for going to college was to play baseball, but his time at Miami resulted in much more.

Jimmy's son — Starting them early ...

It's possible that had he reached out to Stanky and gotten under the tutelage of a major league coach, things would have been different. As it turned out, Jimmy injured his pitching arm while at Miami, ending his professional prospects and aspirational baseball dream.

All wasn't lost by going to Miami instead of going pro out of high school. Between baseball meetings, workouts, practices, and studies, Jimmy had a job working at the girls' dorm. It was there that he met Barb, the girl from Cincinnati, and the two married.

Finished with college, with no hopes of playing pro baseball, and married, it was time to begin a family and career. He first went with what he knew, the printing business, joining the McCall Corporation, printer of thirty-five magazines with headquarters in New York. While working in McCall's personnel department, Jimmy was in charge of several personnel-based functions including human resource activities and McCall's suggestion program, also known as grievances.

After a year of dealing with twelve different employee unions, Jimmy decided to expand his horizons and begin life as a salesman. He worked for a large international company, selling a product he'd never used—saw chain and chainsaw-related items. The company was Omark, with a division in Cincinnati.

Omark took Jimmy and Barb to Raytown, Missouri, located just outside Kansas City and adjacent to Independence, the home of Missouri's President Harry S. Truman. While on his way to the Independence hospital, where Barb delivered a daughter and then later a set of twin girls, Jimmy recalls seeing "give 'em hell," Harry Truman out for walks.

They were only in Kansas City long enough to start a family, make good neighbors, and establish raspberry bushes, when Omark transferred them back to Cincinnati. Soon after the move back, Omark announced a corporate shake-up. Since Jimmy had made a name for himself, a job for him was secure, but it was in a different capacity and a different city. He was offered the sales manager position responsible for the region stretching from Minnesota to New England. It required a move to Hackensack, New Jersey, where they added two boys, one at a time, to the brood of girls.

Omark wasn't the only company making changes. Gordon, impressed with Jimmy—grateful for the Bryan Equipment lead and realizing Jimmy had called on many distributors, seen their operation, and gained the knowledge of what it took to be a genuine distributor—offered Jimmy STIHL for the region of Vermont, New Hampshire, and Maine. Jimmy, realizing the potential in the heavily wooded area, pounced on the opportunity, but with a condition.

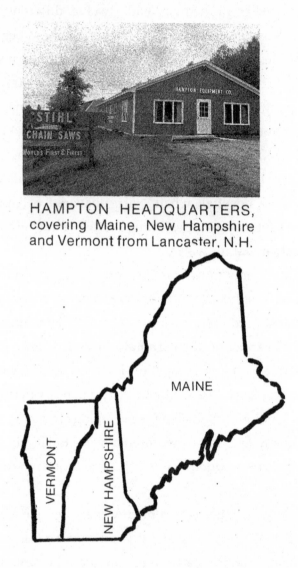

HAMPTON HEADQUARTERS,
covering Maine, New Hampshire
and Vermont from Lancaster, N.H.

Knowing the value of personal relationships, and the need to
have help getting STIHL introduced into the richly wooded but
sparsely populated north woods, Jimmy agreed to become STIHL
American's New England distributor as long as the Omark representative for the area agreed to come on board. One of Jimmy's
best regional managers was then covering the area for Omark. He

was hardworking and well-respected by the dealers. His inten-
sity was such that he literally seldom shut off his station wagon
while making dealer calls. He was known to drive the full length
of Maine simply to respond to the needs of a single dealer. Jimmy
was sure to hit the ground running with the assistance of this key
individual.

The two of them traveled the area and chose Lancaster, New
Hampshire, centrally located in the most densely forested area
of the three-state region, as their headquarters. An already established distributor of noncompetitive products rented office space
to Jimmy and agreed to temporarily handle shipping and receiving. Everything was in place and set to begin operations when
the key person that Jimmy had counted on decided to stay with
Omark. This left the entire traveling and dealer establishment to
Jimmy — now truly a one-man show, albeit with the assistance of
the landlord's small distributor team. With a few pieces of rudimentary literature and a demonstration saw, he hit the road while
Barb tended to their new home, in a new state and new town, and
their five children.

Convincing dealers to take on STIHL when they were already
happy with Homelite or McCulloch, and not wanting to put their
existing dealership in jeopardy, was daunting. Jimmy, used to
being cordially greeted while representing Omark in other areas,
found quite the opposite when attempting to pioneer STIHL in
a competitively established market. Once, when returning to a
dealer where he'd left literature, he learned the dealer had used
the literature to start a stove fire each morning.

Success was slow, but eventually Jimmy convinced a scant
few dealers to try the STIHL. The ones who did told others. One
of the selling techniques he used was the compression demonstra-

tion developed by the whiz kid, showing off STIHL's compression even when the piston rings had been removed. One by one, STIHL began to be accepted throughout New England.

Within a year Jimmy moved the operation to a rented facility with saws and parts in the basement and a couple of offices on the main floor. One of the warehouse workers followed Jimmy and became his lone receiver/shipper/billing department in the basement. A female employee answered the single phone line upstairs. Jimmy hit the road on Monday and returned on Friday, exhausted, and greeted Barb, also exhausted, and their five young kids, who were not exhausted and were eager to enjoy the great outdoors of New Hampshire.

While he spent as many weekends as possible coaching youth sports and participating in community activities, too many weekends were spent away from home at dealer events and county fairs. One of Jimmy's many fond memories of pioneering STIHL is the STIHL-emblazoned pickup he purchased from the legendary Gene Ahlborn. It was a 1965 Dodge equipped with a customized camper shell that opened on both sides and functioned as a traveling display. He rolled into an event, opened the side windows, rolled out the canvas awning, and quickly gathered a curious crowd. In those days most had never heard of STIHL, and nobody knew the correct pronunciation. Some pronounced it "style," others "still," and a scant few got it right—"steel." Jimmy spent many nights away from home in an effort to raise interest in STIHL among the pulp and hardwood cutters in hopes they'd inquire at their local dealer about a STIHL.

The '65 Dodge

Jimmy and Barb have few regrets and many fond memories of pioneering STIHL in New England. It was STIHL that took them to New Hampshire, a delightful place to raise a family. STIHL is now the number-one-selling brand in all of New England. It wasn't that way when the lefty from Ohio came to town. And that distributor from Ohio, the one Jimmy introduced to STIHL, Bryan Equipment; they're still placing record-breaking orders and remain one of STIHL's largest customers. Much of STIHL's success is due to the Hamptons and others like them.

Chapter Twenty-Six

THE TIMES—
THEY WERE A-CHANGIN'

VIRG HATFIELD HAD DONE A masterful job of introducing STIHL to the legendary professional loggers of the great Northwest, home of the world's largest timber forests. With the addition of new models to the line, STIHL was interested in growing their market share beyond just the pure logger, to the farmer, rancher, and firewood cutter. Virg was not interested in dealing with a large number of dealers and simply would not be told what to do.

One of Virg's larger longtime customers, Bill Warren—located nearby in Morton, Washington—was well-known to Al Whyte, STIHL American's regional representative. Bill, his father a farmer and mother a schoolteacher, had grown up in the tall-timber region. He had always been intrigued with the logging industry and chainsaws in particular. His first job was working for a chainsaw dealer. He eventually opened his own chainsaw shop where he sold and serviced saws to area loggers. Remembering his early days of financial struggle, Bill creatively leased STIHLs to young men just getting their start in the logging industry. He had a knack for making money by helping others do the same. He successfully operated the dealership for ten years and was prepared when opportunity knocked.

The relationship between Virg and STIHL American continued to deteriorate. Al Whyte and Rainer Gloeckle, recognizing Bill Warren's aggressive and creative marketing initiative, approached Bill with the prospect of becoming STIHL's distributor for the Northwest. With Bill's immediate and enthusiastic affirmation, Ernie Rainey headed west.

A year or so earlier, Bill had hired Jim Nanny, fresh out of Morton High School. Recognizing Jim's exceptional technical skills and the potential for him to help grow the business, Bill made Jim a minor partner. Bill and Jim, in anticipation of Ernie's visit, began formalizing a plan to realize their dream of becoming a wholesale distributor for STIHL. The first step was securing necessary financing. The first two banks they approached turned them down, but the third time was the charm.

Ernie's plan was to first meet with Virg and break the news that he was on the way to iron out a deal with Bill Warren. Al Whyte, keenly aware of Ernie's soft heart and Virg's likely ability to change Ernie's mind, convinced Ernie to first meet with Bill.

Bill, Jim, and Ernie met over dinner and struck a verbal agreement. Bill and Jim would be handling all the territory previously covered by Virg Hatfield. Bill, anxious and fearful that the deal was a dream too good to be true, scribbled a contract on a napkin, and all three signed. STIHL's new distributor would be aptly named—STIHL Northwest.

Ernie then broke the news to Virg, but with a contract already signed, albeit on a napkin, there was no turning back.

STIHL Northwest quickly moved to the top of the list that ranked distributors by sales volume. In those days heavy logging was in play throughout Washington, Oregon, and Alaska. Bill and Jim established tight service-intensive relationships with all the dealers who serviced major loggers, resulting in STIHL's dominance that continues to this day.

While rapid growth is good, it requires abundant financial capital or creative business processes. Keeping in mind the challenge to get financing, Bill and Jim got creative. Rather than adopt the standard practice of a monthly billing cycle, they used a bimonthly system in which the dealers would settle their accounts twice per month, essentially reducing the funds necessary to handle their accounts receivable by nearly half.

Much like other early STIHL dealers converted to wholesalers, Bill and Jim learned as they went. In the early days everyone answered the phone, filled the orders, and processed the paperwork. Eventually they would move to Chehalis, Washington. They became one of the first distributors with a computer system, a highly trained customer service department, and an efficiently designed warehouse system.

Bill and Jim paid close attention to the changing needs of America's premier loggers, and doing so paid rich dividends. STIHL Northwest's sales volume for both saws and saw chain quickly got the attention of the Stihl family and STIHL Germany executives. Soon, Bill and Jim were invited to visit the factory in Germany on an annual basis to discuss product development. STIHL American applauded Bill and Jim's ability to influence product development in Germany. STIHL Northwest was the first to adopt many products with new enhancements, oftentimes improvements recommended by Bill or Jim. Coaxed by both Al and Fred Whyte, STIHL Northwest became the first distributor to sell STIHL saw chain exclusively.

When Bill and Jim reached retirement age, they worked out a mutually beneficial arrangement with friend and president of STIHL Inc., Fred Whyte, and sold STIHL Northwest to STIHL Incorporated. On July 1, 1994, STIHL Northwest became the first American distributor owned by STIHL.

Chapter Twenty-Seven

TONY BALL

TONY BALL WAS ANOTHER LEGENDARY dynamo who played an instrumental role in STIHL's reintroduction to America. I was unable to find anyone interested in helping with Tony's profile. The following was mined from *Chain Saw Age*, the premier trade publication at the time.

Ball Sales and Service of Mount Morris, Michigan, began selling STIHL in 1958 and covered Michigan. Led by Tony Ball, equally as enthusiastic as neighboring Gene Ahlborn, Ball Sales competed at the Great Lakes Forestry Exhibition, winning cutting contests several years running in the five cubic-inch category. Tony was once quoted as saying, "Michigan pulpwood cutters have taken to STIHLs like women to nylon stockings." Tony's greatest claim to fame is his friendship with the great Gordie Howe of the Detroit Red Wings and appearing on the front cover of *Chain Saw Age*, April 1969, alongside Gordie, holding a STIHL 041AV.

CHAIN SAW AGE

WORLD WIDE SINCE 1952

APRIL 1969

IN THIS ISSUE

Front Cover Story
See Page 3

DETROIT RED WING STAR AND ALL-TIME
HIGH SCORER OF HOCKEY GORDIE HOWE,
AND MICHIGAN STIHL DISTRIBUTOR TONY
BALL "HAM IT UP" FOR NATIONAL ADVER-
TISING SERIES. STORY PAGE 3.

Chapter Twenty-Eight
STIHL AMERICAN
ROAD WARRIORS

SALES ACROSS THE COUNTRY GREW rapidly, and eventually, Gordon realized that Rainer—although a whiz kid—couldn't do it all. Rainer was given a choice of relocating to anywhere in the United States. By then he'd grown very close to Dorsey Glover, a new STIHL distributor in Malvern, Arkansas. Malvern remained Rainer's base until his transfer to Sweden in the summer of 1971. Rainer was frequently referred to as the only German cowboy in captivity. During his seven years in America, Rainer created what would become STIHL's technical services and factory liaison program in America. He became a proud American citizen, a deputy sheriff, gained his pilot license, raised Aberdeen Angus and quarter horses, owned and flew a gyrocopter powered by three STIHL 090s, was frequently seen flying a Cherokee 140, and was perpetually enjoying life in America.

Rapid sales increases created more demand for field representation for STIHL American. Responsibility for calling on distributors across the country was first divided in half, with Rainer taking the area west of the Mississippi. The eastern half was covered by an experienced newcomer, Kenny Johnson.

Kenny Johnson graduated from Graveraet High School in Marquette, Michigan, in 1942. He didn't have any hobbies to speak of. He was one of nine children (see attached photo; he's the curly-haired boy on the right) who all lived in a very small house in Skandia, Michigan. His mother died when he was eight, and his father was killed in a railroad accident when he was sixteen.

Kenny was the first son born to Gust Johnson (1885–1941) and Augusta (Carlson) Johnson (1900–1934) of Skandia, Michigan. He had three older sisters, Viola, Florence, and Ruth; two younger sisters, Marie and Dorothy; and three younger brothers, Mel, Donnie, and Ray. They lived in a home—all eleven of them—ordered from Sears, Roebuck & Company in Chicago. It was delivered to Skandia in a boxcar—all parts, including framing, roofing, siding, inside and outside trim, windows, and doors. His dad built the house on a stone foundation with a full basement. They were connected to electrical service around 1930.

FRED WHYTE
PHIL VOLLMER   KEN HEUBER   KEN JOHNSON   RICK BRYAN

After his mom passed away, Kenny and his brothers took a job cutting cordwood for a neighbor in New Dalton. For two months, June and July, they walked through the woods for over two miles and then cut and piled wood. They were looking forward to earning money for the Fourth of July. Kenny recalled that the mosquitos were thicker than hair on a dog's back. The neighbor never paid them a single penny—a lesson learned the hard way.

Kenny's father would come home on weekends and bake a batch of bread, pies, and cookies to last the kids for a week. In the summer, they would pick all kinds of berries, nuts, apples, and lambs quarters (also known as pigweed, a common leafy weed that tastes like spinach when steamed). They were always hungry.

Kenny walked to Station School, named for its proximity to the Lake Superior and Illinois railroad depot, about a mile-and-a-half away. No roads were plowed back then. They walked mostly on the railroad tracks, which were always plowed by the busy railroad activities.

After moving in with John C. Johnson and his son, George, in the summer of 1936, Kenny learned to be a farmhand. He had to milk cows by hand—no milking machines. That fall, there were ten milking cows and a few head of young stock as well.

By July 1941, at age seventeen, Ken had already made up his mind to go into the navy as soon as he finished school, if not before.

Then on August 29, 1941, his father was killed in a train accident in Champion, Michigan. He was run over by a locomotive in a railroad yard while loading slag ore. The nine children were now orphans. All of his younger siblings were put into foster homes.

Kenny signed up for the navy before he graduated from school in 1943 and was assigned to the *USS West Point*, a 1,200 passenger luxury liner (the *SS America*) converted to carry ten thousand troops. The navy chose it because it was the fastest ship at the time, able to cruise at forty-five knots, over fifty miles per hour! He was honorably discharged in 1945.

That same year, he married Helen Heath and started a chainsaw shop behind his father-in-law's hardware store in Skandia, selling McCulloch chainsaws. Ken and Helen had four children—Judy, Jerry, Keith, and Dana—and lived in a house Ken built in Skandia.

In 1962, Ken was approached by Omark Industries to accept the position of branch manager for their Fort Wayne commercial sales office. He and his entire family, along with a large moving van, were on the road to Fort Wayne, Indiana, when Ken received word that Omark decided to open a branch office in Lansing, Michigan, and positioned him as branch manager there instead. So, he had to contact the moving company to turn the truck around and head back to Lansing, where the family lived for four years.

In 1966 he and Helen moved to Rock Lake—outside of Vest-
aburg and about sixty miles north of Lansing—with their two
youngest sons. Their older son and daughter stayed behind in
Lansing. Ken and Helen lived on the lake for twenty-five years.

When Rainer Gloeckle's territory was cut in half, Ken was contacted by STIHL American to become vice president of sales for the eastern half of America. His youngest son remembers him being so excited about the new job that he was skipping through the house. He remained with STIHL until his retirement in 1990. His last job with the company was as a liability consultant, training lawyers how to use a chainsaw.

In 1991 he and Helen returned to the Upper Peninsula, to an old farmhouse east of Trenary. They lived there for twelve years until 2003, when they moved to Lake Bluff Retirement Village in Gladstone. They lived there until Ken's death in December 2015. His youngest son, Dana, had meanwhile moved back from Oregon where he had been living for twenty-nine years to live with and take care of his aging parents. In a year and a half—from June 2014 to December 2015—Dana drove Ken all over the Upper Peninsula to visit his many friends one last time . . . and sometimes several last times.

After Ken's death, Dana took his mom to Gowen to live with Dana's high school sweetheart Ruth May Sanderson, now a veteran registered nurse. It was her idea for Helen to live with them at her house. Dana and Ruth married on May 5, 2015, and Ken's widow, Helen, still lives with them. Helen goes on many day-long road trips around central Michigan with Dana while Ruth continues to work as a nurse in Grand Rapids.

It's nearly impossible to imagine Kenny having any spare time, but he found time to build Helen a giant dollhouse. The house now sits at Peter White Library in Marquette, Michigan.

Chapter Twenty-Nine
BOB VAN SCHELVEN

PRODUCT DEVELOPMENT CONTINUED, AND THE number of saws offered continued to expand. More saws, more business, and more dealers resulted in greater demand for field representation. Meanwhile, Rainer was needed in Europe. Coinciding with Rainer's departure from the United States was the addition of two field representatives: one a newlywed fresh out of the University of Iowa and the other an experienced veteran. Both were already known to Gordon, and it's thought their job interviews were a mere formality.

Bob Van Schelven was born 1932 in Grand Haven, Michigan, the youngest of three boys. After earning a record-setting nine varsity letters in football, basketball, and baseball—while a diminutive 130 pounds wringing wet—he attended Western Michigan University in Kalamazoo. Immediately following graduation from college, he married sweet Caroline; they'd been dating since high school.

Bob began his working career in Grand Haven with a locally known and worldwide provider of industrial tools—Gardner-Denver. An advancement with Gardner required a move to New Jersey where he and Caroline remained for nearly forty years. Always the avid athlete, Bob rekindled his love of sports by coaching Pop Warner football. One of the many players Bob coached, mentored, and inspired was Craig Williams, son of Gordon Williams.

Sales of STIHL products had blossomed exponentially all over America, particularly in the Northeast. Realizing the importance of nurturing a business relationship, Gordon Williams made the decision to add a field representative in order to better serve the STIHL distributors and dealers in the Northeast.

After more than fifteen years with Gardner-Denver, Bob was ready for a change. Already familiar with the Williams family through Craig, Bob made it known that he was interested in the position. Gordon put Bob through the formality of a job interview, but after seeing Bob's natural talent of for dealing with people— adolescent football players and their parents—he knew he was the man for the job.

It's possible that Gordon felt an obligation to give Bob a chance as a way of repaying him for so many years as a volunteer coach. It's more likely that it was the combination of Bob's experience with Gardner-Denver and his exhibited diplomacy while coaching that earned him the position with STIHL American. No matter the decision-making process, Bob remained with STIHL until his retirement in 1989. He and Gordon had both made the right decision.

During Bob's tenure at STIHL, he set the example of an exceptional regional representative. While he was employed by and represented STIHL, he did whatever it took to make sure all members of the channel, STIHL, the distributor, the dealer, and even the customer were satisfied with the product. He was truly a long-ball hitter and a prankster.

Bob and the newbie college kid came on board at nearly the same time. At their first STIHL meeting, the college kid was rooming with his father, also an employee of STIHL. During the first day's meeting, the newbie complained about his father's snoring while bragging about the solution, moving his mattress onto the room's balcony. Bob's room was conveniently located just one floor above the newbie. The next morning, while enjoying the soothing sounds of ocean waves rather than the disruptive snoring of a father suffering from sleep apnea, the newbie was surprised by a pitcher of ice cold water from the balcony above.

The newbie owes Bob a true debt of gratitude because there must be something inspiring about being awoken by a cold pitcher of water during one's inaugural STIHL sales meeting. The newbie, Fred Whyte, went on to become STIHL Incorporated's longest serving and most successful president, and Bob's boss.

Chapter Thirty

FRED WHYTE

FOR TWENTY YEARS ETTA WHYTE waited at home each night for her husband's safe return. Al Whyte, a graduate of the Royal Canadian Mounted Police School—comparable to America's advanced FBI training—served on Vancouver, British Columbia's police force for over twenty years before joining Titan Chainsaw Company. Al was Titan's sales engineer responsible for Washington, Idaho, and Montana. Since the new position was with an American company and working in America, Al, Etta, and their eight-year-old son moved a few miles south, across the Washington state line.

After gaining considerable knowledge of the chainsaw and timber industry while serving Titan, McCulloch, and Homelite, Al was hired by STIHL American to cover America's Northwest, the world's greatest timber region.

Al and Etta's only son, Fred, watched and learned. During Fred's undergraduate college summers, he interned at Homelite's northwest branch office. It was a foretelling beginning.

As is the case with all honorable Scotsmen, Fred mastered the bagpipes, simply referred to as pipes by true Scotsmen. By the time he graduated from college, Fred had competed in and won several piping contests; the consequence was an offer from the University of Iowa for a staff teaching position and an opportunity to earn his master's degree.

Young Fred Whyte making his first cut with a Titan

The University of Iowa's pipe band had a long-running tradition. When the enrollment of pipe playing men dwindled during World War II, the university created an all-women's pipe band. Fred's teaching position was not awarded in order for him to play the pipes but rather for him to direct the world's largest all-girls pipe band, 150 members strong. One of his students, only a couple of years younger than he, first caught his eye and then his heart.

When Fred and Karen were newlyweds—he just having completed an introductory sales training curriculum with Datsun of

America and Karen just settling into her position as the county nurse—Fred received a life-changing phone call from his father, Al. Opportunity was tapping at their door. Rainer Gloeckle, who Fred's father had succeeded in the Northwest, was leaving Arkansas and returning to Germany. Al encouraged Fred to apply for the position.

In 1971 most had yet to hear about STIHL, and those who had couldn't properly pronounce the name. A typical dealer display consisted of a three-saw rack with two of the saws used and dripping oil. STIHL was recognized and highly praised by many professional loggers, but STIHL's market share was likely in the single digits. STIHL was nowhere near the leading brand it is today.

It's possible that Fred had at one time begrudged his father for being forced to learn the pipes, but if so, he surely realized that it was the pipes that led him to Karen. All things considered, Fred realized his father usually knew what he was doing and did it for good reason. He had fond memories of the time he'd spent working at Homelite as an intern. To top off the series of events that had taken place over the course of several years, Fred had used one of STIHL's newest models, the S10, during a recent visit with his parents. Fred and Karen rightly concluded it prudent to take Al's advice and at least apply.

Fred flew to New Jersey for the interview. Gordon Williams picked him up at the airport in his 600 Mercedes Benz. Fred recalls getting stares while receiving the royal treatment and then getting into a Mercedes limousine. It's not likely that any of Fred's University of Iowa master's program classmates would be treated to an interview such as the one Fred was about to attend. Rather than check into a hotel, Gordon took Fred to his home to meet his family. While watching a preseason NFL football game, the first American man of STIHL, Ernie Rainey, joined them.

Based on what each had heard about the other through Fred's father, it was almost as if they'd already met. Judging by the evening's agenda, it's plausible to think that Gordon had decided to offer Fred the job days earlier. Knowing that Fred was a Scotsman, they plied him with Johnny Walker Black Label Scotch. Fred remembers little else about the evening except getting lost in the house between his bedroom and the toilet.

Fred had the good sense to speak to Karen before accepting the offer. After agreeing to embark on the new adventure together, they rented a U-Haul and headed south toward Little Rock, Arkansas. Even though Fred followed the legendary whiz kid, he brought his own unique style and quickly established his own identity within the STIHL culture.

I recall one of Fred's first sales meetings at Crader. The sales team had gathered at a remote cabin on the banks of a spring-fed southern Missouri river. Fred arose early the first morning and quietly crept away before anyone noticed he was gone. Just when the sun began to cast a few faint shadows and everyone had gathered on the cabin's screened-in porch, Fred emerged from the fog in his pipe-playing regalia, marching to the eerie sound of "Scotland The Brave." The first response was to take a shot at the mysterious person in the questionable garb, followed by curiosity as to the undergarments one wears while playing the pipes. Fred plowed his own furrow.

In Fred's case, the blessing of the father was visited upon the son. Fred and Karen's union produced a son and a daughter, John and Jean. Like Fred, John was eager to learn to play the pipes. And like Fred, he excelled. Fred and John eventually competed in

Scotland's Annual World Championship Pipe Band Competition where they placed third out of fifty-two bands.

STIHL continued to enjoy rapid growth and record-setting sales years. Fred's field position was eventually split into multiple regions taken over by others when he moved to Virginia Beach as a product manager for guide bars and saw chain. It was during that time when most STIHL distributors began selling STIHL chain exclusively and abandoned brands such as Carlton and Oregon.

Appropriately impressed with Fred's leadership abilities, the Stihl family asked Fred to first establish and then lead a Canadian operation, where he'd be responsible for distribution of STIHL throughout all of Canada. Fred's performance in Canada resulted in him being asked to return to Virginia Beach as President of STIHL Inc., responsible for marketing, sales, and the rapid expansion of STIHL's North American manufacturing operations.

After serving STIHL for over forty-five years and leading the company from a moderately known brand to America's biggest-selling outdoor handheld power tool, Fred retired as STIHL Incorporated's longest-serving president. The Stihl family, not wishing to lose Fred's knowledge and influence, appointed him sole director and chairman of the board at STIHL Inc.—a board of one, created solely to keep Fred in the game.

During the research for this book, I had the privilege of spending an afternoon with Fred and Karen at their home in Virginia Beach. He and I discussed the book and reminisced about all things STIHL: the Stihl family, STIHL's unique marketing strategy, what STIHL had meant to my family and so many others, and regretfully, Fred's recent diagnosis with cancer. Just before Karen graciously drove me back to my hotel, I shook Fred's hand, patted him on the shoulder, and confirmed that I'd pray for him. We both knew it was likely our last earthly visit. Fred passed away soon thereafter on July 7, 2017. His passing left me with a wounded heart that won't soon—if ever—be healed.

Fred with Fergie and Hogan

Chapter Thirty-One

DEALERS CHOOSE STIHL

STIHLS DON'T SELL THEMSELVES; THEY never did, and they never will. STIHL's commitment to product quality backed up by expert customer service will always be the primary tenent in STIHL's strategy. No matter the ingenuity of the market strategy, STIHL's success has been dependent on product quality and the servicing dealer. It's the dealer who represents the last ten feet in the long channel, beginning with a chunk of raw material to the creation of a part that is used to assemble the product and eventually making its way to the dealer's display. When the customer walks through the door, it's the dealer who decides if all the effort put forth up until that point bears fruit. Even though it's the product quality that keeps the customer satisfied and sustains the relationship, the dealer will always play an essential and critical role. The following are examples of the kinds of dealers who, by providing dedicated customer service, have contributed to STIHL's unparalleled success.

Chapter Thirty-Two

WINE COUNTRY

MISSOURI'S RHINELAND LIES ALONG THE last hundred-mile stretch of America's longest river, the mighty Missouri. Big Mo begins twenty-three hundred miles upstream at the confluence of the Jefferson, Madison, and Gallatin Rivers, near Three Forks, Montana. While the French were the first Europeans to explore and establish settlements along the entire length of the river, German immigrants, following soon thereafter, settled primarily along the last hundred miles between Jefferson City, Missouri's capital, and Saint Louis, where the Missouri flows into the Mississippi.

The most well-known village along this stretch is Hermann, named in honor of Hermann Arminius, chieftain of the German Cherusci tribe—the German warrior whose armies defeated three of Caesar Augustus's legions in the Battle of the Teutoburg Forest. Most Hermann settlers weren't warriors; the most practical skill they brought with them from the old country was that of growing excellent grapes for the making of award-winning wine. Within ten years following the arrival of the Germans, the Hermann area became one of the world's largest wine-making regions. A little-known fact outside of Missouri is that during the 1851 Vienna World's Fair, Missouri wines took eight of the twelve gold medals. The French weren't happy, especially considering the wine was made from a grape unique to America, the Norton. (Coincidentally, the Norton grape was discovered in Virginia, not far from STIHL's eventual North American headquarters.)

Never to be bested by America, the French grafted Norton rootstock from the World's Fair champion vineyards, which were growing abundantly on the steep Missouri River valley hillsides. Unbeknownst to the French, the grafted rootstock carried a root louse that had no affect while growing in the Missouri Rhineland, but once in France, spread to vineyards native to Europe. It became a plague and nearly destroyed vineyards across all of France and other parts of Europe.

A pair of Missourians discovered the malady, and an estimated ten million cured rootstocks were shipped from Missouri to Europe, saving the French wine industry. In a show of appreciation and recognition, the French bestowed the Cross of the Legion of Honor and the Order of Knighthood on one of the men responsible for saving France's vineyards. Why they didn't knight both is a mystery.

Missourians of German ancestry enjoy claiming to have saved the French wine industry almost as much as they like to take credit for the rootstock that was transplanted from Missouri to France and then later to California. French sommeliers know the truth and will admit it when questioned; few Californians will concede. This author's favorite wine is that which is on sale, and I have been known to drink wine from a bottle, box, or Mason jar.

Chapter Thirty-Three
THE GOLD STANDARD

CHAMOIS, MISSOURI, IS LOCATED JUST downstream from where the Osage River flows into the Missouri, and a few miles upstream from Hermann. Chamois was named after Chamonix, France, due to its Alpine scenery, steep, forested hillsides, and lush river-bottom valleys—and the fact that the French were first in that area. While the village is named for the French, the inhabitants are clearly of German descent and culture. And so, it makes sense that the local chainsaw dealer would sell STIHL.

Like so many of that era, Alphonse and Hugo Brandt were loggers first and chainsaw retailers second. In those days a logger wouldn't think of buying a saw from someone who didn't know saws. How would one know saws without first having used one? Once Alphonse and Hugo tired of cutting staves, they decided to open a small business selling tires, guns, and saws. The only qualification necessary to sell tires in those days was good credit and the grit and stamina to change tires on cars, trucks, and tractors. They had both. The only additional qualification necessary to sell saws was the intelligence and skill to repair them and the willingness to do so at all hours of the day. Again, Hugo and Alphonse were more than qualified. They set the gold standard for customer service. And their sons continue to do so today.

The Brandt brothers, with little more than an eighth grade education—but a lifetime of learning and gifted with uncommon

common sense—officially started their business in 1962 and cleverly named the enterprise Brandt Chainsaw. It was never a question of customers finding their business because everyone knew where it was: at Hugo's house. Hugo's house is located at the end of a long, gravel, creek-crossing driveway a few miles from Chamois. Since they'd been using Remington saws, they first chose Remington as the brand to sell.

Kathryn, Alphonse, Rita, and Hugo Brandt

Their reputation of integrity and expertise was widely known. Numerous vendors began calling on them and offering them dealerships on a variety of timber and farm-related products. The brothers chose to stay in their lane, so to speak, and focus on selling items that they could sell and service without making a significant capital investment—tires, saws, belts, and several small wear items. They'd only been in business a few months when a vendor salesman, who also represented STIHL in another area, suggested they consider STIHL saws, explaining how a Remington was really a Mall and a Mall simply a copy of a STIHL. STIHL was the real deal. The brothers contacted their local STIHL distributor, Don Crader, and today, they claim the call to be one of the most important calls in the history of their fifty-plus year success story.

By late 1962 the STIHL 07 was in production, the first STIHL model sold by the Brandt brothers. It was an excellent seller for them until introduction of the 08, a much lighter—albeit slightly less powerful—unit. They quickly became the largest STIHL dealer in Missouri, and possibly the largest sellers of chainsaws of any brand in Missouri. While the 07 was a more powerful machine, the Brandts pushed people toward the 08 because of its unparalleled power-per-pound feature, which turned out to be a good move.

They had sold over two hundred chainsaws by the time a technical problem with the 07, an issue fairly unique to southern Missouri, reared its ugly head. During hot and humid conditions, the units were difficult or impossible to restart after having run a full tank of gas. Immediately after learning of the problem, Don Crader and Rainer, the whiz kid, spent several days with the Brandt brothers and their customers diagnosing the problem. They determined the problem to be vapor locking, a condition where the fuel is heated to the point that it becomes a gas and can't be pulled into the saw's fuel system. The fact that STIHL sent their top person to the scene endeared STIHL to the Brandts, and likewise the Brandts to their customers, who'd grown accustomed to being abandoned by manufacturers when a technical problem arose. Eventually, the vapor-locking problem occurred in other areas, but by then, thanks to the patient cooperation of the Brandts and STIHL's quick reaction, a fix had been determined and was available.

Over the years Rainer returned many times to the Brandts. When he'd learned of users experiencing a problem with a saw, he'd want to know if the same was occurring with the Brandt customers. And if so, he'd return to Chamois and work with the Brandt brothers to diagnose the issue. He did this for a couple of reasons. The Brandts had a knack for precisely describing the problem and the conditions under which it occurred. But most of all, Rainer enjoyed their hospitality. A visit to the Brandt operation always resulted in dinner with the entire family, some of whom could still speak a little German. To this day, Rainer recalls seeing a chicken running around the barnyard during the morning and being served that evening for dinner. "Now that's farm fresh," Rainer used to boast.

In those days chain clinics were a popular draw. Loggers and farmers would pile into Brandt's shop building in hopes of learning the art of saw-chain sharpening. There would always be a blazing fire in the wood-burning stove, located in the center of the room. Since the shop had a dirt floor, the walls didn't extend all the way to the ground. To say the room had a draft is an under-statement, but nobody complained. They were there to learn how to properly sharpen a saw chain. The Brandts bought into the Chinese proverb about teaching a man to fish . . . and realized that people would be more satisfied with their saws if the chain was sharp. They had traded for many a fine saw that the owner thought worthless due to a dull chain.

During the early days, Crader Distributing always had a booth at Missouri's State Fair. (Recall that STIHL was still a brand in its infancy in America.) Most coming through the booth had heard very little of STIHL. A map was always kept on display to show people the location of their nearest dealer. Owners of a STIHL would be asked where they'd made their purchase. The Brandts always held the record for people having driven the furthest to purchase a STIHL. The statement frequently repeated was that they'd gone to Chamois hearing of the good prices on saws but returned because of the quality service and genuine hospitality. More than a few had driven over a hundred miles, passing several dealers along the way, simply to enjoy the Brandt experience. Today, fathers from all over the Midwest are taking their sons to the place where their father introduced them to STIHL — Chamois, Missouri.

When asked to share a memory of the early days selling STIHL, Rita tells the story of how, after regular business hours, Hugo and Alphonse would work on saws in their basement, which was also where the washing machine was. So, she'd have to wait until Hugo was finished working on saws, sometimes after midnight, before doing the laundry and then hanging it out to dry, sometimes only a few hours before daylight. When asked if Hugo ever started the saws in the basement, Rita just laughed and said, "oh, yes," waving her hand in front of her nodding head, "And the fumes!" The Brandt kids grew up living and literally breathing STIHL; STIHL is in their blood.

Every family has their handed-down stories. The Brandts have a doozey. It was handed down by Rita's father, Joe Keilholz. It was about 1925 when Joe, while working one of his Missouri River bottom fields, heard a familiar sound, a sputtering engine, but it was coming from an unfamiliar place, the sky. Joe watched while the pilot landed the belching plane safely in a nearby field and then he curiously but cautiously approached. It turned out to be a de Havilland DH4 mail plane with a fouled spark plug. As luck would have it, for the pilot, Joe had a car and took the pilot into town, where he caught the next train into Saint Louis. A few days later, the pilot returned with new spark plugs, got the plane running, and offered Joe a ride for his trouble. Joe told the pilot he thought it best to make sure the plane was running well before going for a ride. The pilot grinned and understood. He took down Joe's phone number. Joe was evidently well-to-do, judging from the fact that he had both a car and a telephone.

Several weeks later the pilot called and let Joe know he'd be flying that same route again, that the plane was running fine, and the offer for a ride was still good. This time Joe agreed and placed a large, white mattress sheet in the field with the smoothest turf. That afternoon the pilot cruised up the river, found the field with the sheet, landed, and took Joe for his first and last airplane ride. Joe and the pilot became friends for life.

Joe Keilholz and Charles Lindbergh

A year or so later that same pilot invited Joe to a party to be held in Saint Louis. The party was in celebration of the first solo transatlantic flight. The mail carrier pilot, you see, had been Charles Lindbergh.

Business school libraries are full of books on best practices, sales and marketing techniques, advertising, promotions, and all things taught and thought necessary to be successful in business. Most benefit from all that has been written and is being taught; however, it's doubtful that a Brandt would benefit from any of this teaching because they're naturals at doing that which results in success. The Brandts know that if they take care of the customer, the customer will take care of them. Word of mouth only works when customers are motivated to share an experience. Brandt experiences are shared by all. They do unto others what they know is the right thing to do with no expectation that the favor will be returned. They chose STIHL over fifty years ago. Dealers such as the Brandts and their loyalty to the brand, and STIHL's loyalty to them, are a significant reason STIHL is number one today. Just as Missouri wine was the gold standard for wine, and STIHL is the gold standard in power tools, the Brandt family is the gold standard for full-service dealers.

The most common comment made about the Brandts is that they're always smiling. People see, and generally find, that for which they're looking. The Brandts look for and find joy. They love STIHL, and STIHL loves them.

Chapter Thirty-Four

SERVICE SELLS

IF THERE HAD BEEN HYPHENATED Americans in the twenties, Greg Bobeen would have been born a Bohemian-American, but as it was, he was simply born an American in 1925 in Troy, Missouri—long before the rhapsody made famous by the rock band Queen hit the charts celebrating Bohemian heritage.

Greg was born into a family of farmers and would have grown up to be a farmer had it not been for the Great Depression, which cost his family the farm. Having completed the ninth grade and learned all he felt he needed to accomplish his life goals and provide for his struggling family, he began delivering ice for a local ice company. Since Missouri's electric cooperative, founded in 1937, had only begun to reach small towns and had yet to provide service to rural areas, most homes were equipped with an icebox, which depended on a large block of ice to keep perishables cool. Greg enjoyed his time as an ice delivery truck driver and met many who would later become his customers.

By 1943 electric service was more widely available, ice boxes were gradually being replaced by refrigerators, ice-delivery business was waning, and America was at war. Greg enlisted in the navy and served the United States as a navy corpsman, primarily in Saipan, until war's end.

Greg's Saw Center

Following an honorable discharge from the navy, Greg returned to Troy and found work managing a local two-bay Texaco Service Station. The owner made it clear to Greg that he planned to eventually hand the filling station over to his son, who would soon be graduating from high school. Drafted soon after high school graduation, the owner's son headed for Korea. Greg was to manage the station until the owner's son returned. The war experience rendered the owner's son unable to properly manage the station. Once again, with the bad comes the good. Rather than turn the station over to the son, the owner chose to sell the business to Greg.

Greg's son, Paul, shared the story of how his father met his mother, Mary Ann. Greg was on a double date with his girlfriend (not Mary Ann) and her brother with his date (Mary Ann). The details are no longer known, but Greg saw Mary Ann home, and his date and her brother found themselves single again. As it turned out, Mary Ann and Greg had attended the same grade school, but since she was a few years younger, they'd never met. She too had Bohemian ancestry. They were meant to be.

Married, and then the owner of a filling station, Greg took the initiative to supplement the service station's revenue. Since there was an abundance of logging operations nearby, Greg began selling McCulloch chainsaws. After selling only twenty chainsaws the first year and providing unparalleled customer service to the professional loggers, the word got out, and Greg sold nearly two hundred saws the second year. McCulloch proved to be a popular brand of saw for several years and established Greg as the chainsaw dealer preferred by professionals throughout northeastern Missouri.

Paul and Lance hold the first STIHL 090 sold at Greg's

Revenue generated by small engines eventually exceeded that generated by traditional filling station services. Greg took on additional lines of chainsaws and for a short time offered other power tools as well—including mowers, tillers, and go-karts.

In 1967 one of their loyal logging customers began asking about STIHL. Greg, having already proven that he wasn't opposed to trying a new brand, contacted Don Crader, the local STIHL distributor. Greg placed the minimum order to become a dealer, three saws, and sold the first one to the Prater Brothers of Moscow Mills. Once other loggers saw what the Praters were using, the other two saws sold soon after.

By 1971 the power equipment business, originally intended as a supplement, had far eclipsed Greg's expectation. With the intention of slowing down and reducing his workload, Greg moved to a small but more suitable location on the outskirts of town, named the business Greg's Chainsaw Center, and began selling only chainsaws: STIHL, Homelite, and McCulloch.

In spite of Greg's intentions to semiretire and slow down, the business continued to grow. Rather than slowly reducing the volume of business in his small one-man shop, his focus on chainsaws resulted in Greg's Saw Center becoming one of the leading shops for chainsaw sales in the northeastern quarter of Missouri. By 1976 Greg decided that the only way out was to sell, but just as with his plans to settle slowly into retirement fifteen years earlier, the business wouldn't be sold.

Paul, the third of Greg and Mary Ann's four children, then attending Truman State University, had spent too many days at the shop during his formative years to see it go. He temporarily left Truman to help out a few days and never returned. Like his father before him, he'd learned enough to be successful.

Instead of coming home from college with a degree, Paul returned with a wife, Paula, whom he had met during his years at Truman. Paula began a noble career as a teacher, while Paul began his with the greatest mentor a man could ask for: his father. Greg passed away in 2007 leaving behind an enduring legacy.

Forty years after moving to the preretirement location where Greg planned to dial things back, Greg's Chain Saw Center sells STIHL and STIHL accessories exclusively. Paul's nephew, Lance, spent many Saturdays at the shop sweeping and cleaning, in exchange for two Kennedy half-dollars; he still has all of them. He joined Paul in the business, doubling the size of the staff. Paul and Lance, a two-man show, sell nearly a thousand units a year and continue to service units sold decades earlier.

During my visit at Greg's while gathering information for this story, a longtime customer appeared with a brand X saw purchased new in 1971 that needed the chain sharpened. Lance sharpened the chain while the customer bragged about STIHL and made sure that Paul and Lance realized that the forty-five-year-old Homelite was used only on stumps. Ironically, the model of saw, Homelite EZ, matched the saw featured on one of the legacy outdoor signs, likely the same age as the saw.

Chapter Thirty-Five

THE FIRST NONTRADITIONAL STIHL DEALER

IN THE ERA OF BIG box chain stores and Amazon.com, small independent shops struggle to compete. For every rule there is an exception. Greg's Saw Center is an outstanding exception. There's every reason to believe the two-man shop will be successful well into the third generation, selling STIHL exclusively.

Not every big box store is the same. STIHL proved it was possible to do business with the traditional small engine shops as well as the large general merchandise stores, so long as core principles weren't compromised.

Just as with Andreas Stihl, who invented the chainsaw after recognizing the need, a few mid-American independent businessmen saw a need and took action. Recognizing the buying power that the national branded chain stores such as JCPenney, Western Auto, Sears, and others enjoyed, and the effect it was having on their businesses, two groups—almost simultaneously—devised a buying-power plan of their own. The two groups, known today as Mid-States and Wheatbelt, had separate roots in North Dakota. Created respectively in 1954 and 1955, they were initially dealing primarily in automotive parts. By the mid-1960s the Wheatbelt buying group included more than forty stores when they decided to expand the stores to a full complement of general merchandise, including farm items, animal health, automotive, clothing and footwear, hardware, housewares, lawn and garden, paint, pet supplies, plumbing and electrical, saddle and tack, sporting goods, and toys.

While each member store enjoys the opportunity to combine their needs and gain better pricing through large volume purchases, each store is independently owned and managed. It's not unusual to see a brand offered in one store and not in another— which was and is the case with STIHL. When Crader Distributing salesman John Dillard noticed STIHL losing market share in an area served by Louie's Farm & Home of Warrensburg, Missouri, he investigated.

Louie Feldman, a local farmer, and Ray Swisher, a local grain elevator owner, had partnered to open Louie's Farm & Home. Ray's older brother, Max, is likely the father of the popular zero-turn riding mower. And it's possible that Louie's Farm & Home sold the very first zero-turn riding mower in the world. Ray's brother, Max, in an effort to produce an economically priced

riding mower, designed and manufactured a small rider, which
at one point was sold by nearly all Wheatbelt associates—Louie's
likely being the first to sell one.

Louie and John Dillard, cut from similar bolts of cloth comprised with threads of independence, didn't hit it off immediately.
John, determined to make STIHL number one, persisted until
Louie agreed to John's terms—which were Crader's terms—which
essentially called for Louie to offer service. Louie didn't admit it at
first, but the STIHLs were easier to sell, and customers were more
satisfied with their purchase than any other brand of chainsaw.

Louie and Ray hired and trained the best to manage their
store. Once a manager exhibited all the skills necessary to manage
all aspects of the store, they partnered with him or her and established stores in other markets—the first manager being Bill Hash,
with a store in Lebanon, Missouri the next being Ken Hunsperger
in Miami, Oklahoma.

In 1971, Louie, his brother, Larry Parks, and Dan Feldman,
Louie's son, established a Farm & Home store in Odessa, Missouri,
just outside Kansas City. A few years later, nearly the same group

opened Farm & Home of Blue Springs, gradually working their way closer to Kansas City. STIHL soon followed.

Two essential criteria followed along with STIHL to each of the Feldman-inspired stores that allowed the relationship to flourish: service and profit. Dan Feldman, leading by example, proved that the STIHL brand could draw traffic while being sold at the manufactured suggested retail price and that a profit could be generated while offering service after the sale. With Dan's endorsement and advice on price point and service, other Wheatbelt associates expressed an interest in STIHL. As market conditions allowed, additional Wheatbelt stores were added to the quickly growing list of STIHL dealers.

Eventually, the Mid-States associates followed a similar route, likely inspired by the example set by Dan Feldman. At the time of this writing, the Farm & Home category, including both the Wheatbelt and Mid-States groups—with more than a thousand stores nationwide, fifty thousand employees, and over $10 billion in sales—are a leading category for STIHL nationally and represent nearly a quarter of sales for Crader Distributing.

Feldman's is now well into the third generation, with Dan's daughter, Sahrene, at the helm. She has proven to be just as innovative, tenacious, persistent, and customer-service oriented as her father and grandfather.

Stan presenting Dan Feldman with a STIHL carbon fiber guide bar.
L-R: Kyle Kramer, Stan Crader, Dan Feldman, Sahrene and
Alan Buckwalter

Chapter Thirty-Six

THE STORIES NEVER END

THE AUGUST 1965 ISSUE OF *Chain Saw Age* lists the forty-seven distributors representing STIHL at that time. Unlike today—when we
have a relatively homogenous group whose facilities and organi-
zations are very similar and who deliver similar services in their
respective coverage area—the distributors representing STIHL in
1965 included rental yards, logging companies, farm equipment
dealerships, and only a few businesses in which wholesale was
their primary focus. By 2015, fifty years later, through mergers
and acquisitions, the eclectic forty-seven was reduced to ten
highly efficient world-class distributors focused exclusively on
STIHL.

The Andreas Stihl Story

Stihl Distributors Blanket The United States

Ahlborn Equipment Co.
Sayner, Wisconsin

Aldridge Power Mower Co.
Durham, N. C.

Ball Sales and Service
Mount Morris, Mich.

Jack "Chief" Beatty Co.
Denver, Colorado

Brady Saw Mill Supply
Gassaway, W. Va.

Richard Cone
Fort Madison, Iowa

J. C. Cannon
Clinton, S. C.

Crader Distributing Co.
Marble Hill, Mo.

Dakota Wood Products Co.
Bottineau, N. D.

H. C. Davis Forestry Supply
Jackson's Gap, Ala.

Farm and Forest, Inc.
Cincinnati, Ohio

Forestry Equipment Co.
Jacksonville, Fla.
    and
Waycross, Ga.

Art Gary
Canton, New York

W. L. Goodman
Perry, Fla.

Guillaume Saw Service
Baton Rouge, La.

Gulf Coast Distributors
Biloxi, Miss.

Gustin Gardens
Rockville, Md.

Dan Ingersoll
Chestertown, Md.

Imported Motor Sales
Minneapolis, Minn.

Interstate Distributing Co.
Chehalis, Washington
Hood River, Oregon
    and
Weippe, Idaho

Cliff Jones Chain Saw Sales
Montague City, Mass.

Julian Tool and Fuel Co.
Julian, California

L-M Equipment Co.
Portland, Oregon

Ralph A. Laubach
Millerstown, Penna.

Meier and White Eqpt. Co.
Atlanta, Georgia

Midway Distributing Co.
Chico, California

Jim Miller
Phillipsburg, Montana

Joseph N. Minarik
East Paterson, N. J.

Montgomery's Mill Supply
Delta, Pa.

W. W. Morton
Spotsylvania, Va.

Ozark Equipment Co.
Rolla, Mo.

Petersen's Sales and Service
Effie, Mich.

Power Tool Co.
Johnson City, Tenn.

Power Tool Distributing Co.
Luling, Texas

Reade Electric Eqpt. Co.
Walterboro, S. C.

The Red Bird Supply
Tulsa, Okla.

Reynold's Sports
Paris, Tenn.

Ross-Frazier Supply Co.
St. Joseph, Mo.

Selma Cycle and Marine
Selma, Alabama

Stihl Western
Pasadena, Calif.

J. Sherman Tanner
Juneau, Alaska

United Welding Co.
Wellington, Ohio

Ward Bros. Chain Saw Supply
Malvern, Ark.

Waterbury Power Eqpt. Co.
Waterbury, Conn.

Whiting Distributing Co.
Pulaski, Pa.

Wisconsin Midstate Dist. Div.
Mauston, Wis.

The Wright Co.
Tupelo, Miss.

Chapter Thirty-Seven
PEOPLE MAKE THE DIFFERENCE

STIHL AMERICAN WAS DISSOLVED IN the early 1970s, and STIHL Inc. was created. STIHL Parts continued to provide parts service to STIHL distributors for another decade. Fred Whyte was one of two people employed at STIHL Inc. who were part of the STIHL American/STIHL Parts era. The other was Jim Zuidema, whose retirement day at STIHL was in June 2017. Jim was the last member of the era of those profiled in this story.

Jim Zuidema, another Jersey boy, attended Virginia Tech with the intention of becoming a US Air Force pilot. After receiving orders to report for pilot training following commissioning, the need for additional pilots suddenly changed with the ending of hostilities in Vietnam. In April 1973, just prior to graduation/commissioning, he was told his services would not be required after all, and he was discharged from his contract with the Air Force. Not knowing just what to do, in December 1973—while waiting for a better offer—he took a job in the warehouse at STIHL Parts. But while there he came to know the people of STIHL Parts and STIHL American.

He didn't know exactly why, but he sensed something unique, energetic, optimistic, and genuinely altruistic about the people with whom he worked. While he realized the purpose of the enterprise was profit, he witnessed a team of people whose first priority was assuring their customers' success. He was surrounded by a mix of visionaries, flamboyant marketers, and finicky technicians, all focused on a common goal: selling a product, the demand for which always outstripped supply. Jim recalls sensing something great was in the offing, and he decided to hang around a year or so to see how it all worked out.

He eventually became the warehouse and traffic manager of STIHL Parts and, after over forty-two years with STIHL, retired as the supervisor of technical customer service at STIHL Incorporated. He looks back with no regrets. While Jim realizes the success of STIHL hinges on the quality of the product, the people were the draw, making life and work interesting. Like so many others, Jim was right.

Chapter Thirty-Eight
BEGINNING, MIDDLE, BEYOND

THE STIHL AMERICAN STORY BEGAN in Switzerland, took shape in Germany, gained momentum in a rented warehouse in New Jersey, and is now America's best-selling outdoor handheld power tool. STIHL's worldwide operations and ownership is in the third generation, as are STIHL's largest American distributors. The journey began when one man designed a device to make work easier and better for others. Now supported by a research and development staff of over six hundred highly trained and focused engineers, the STIHL innovative drive and success continues. Andreas Stihl set the sales and marketing standard with his many worldwide travels, including the legendary crisscross trek across Canada. That tenacity is now emulated by hundreds of territory managers all across America. STIHL's success is due to the right people in the right place at the right time, selling and supporting a superior product. Quality products sold and supported by quality people is STIHL's simple secret formula for success.

The dealer appreciation trips, like my 1966 trip to Germany, continue to this day. During the fall of 2017, several Crader Distributing dealers were treated to a trip that included a tour through Southern Germany and Western Switzerland. In June

2018, American STIHL distributors will convene in Salzburg, Austria, to begin a lavish tour through the Austrian, Swiss, and German Alps.

STIHL is the world's first and finest, in more ways than one.

Epilogue

Fred Whyte was highly respected by all who knew him, particularly members of the STIHL team. As the longest serving president of STIHL Incorporated, Fred was instrumental in STIHL's climb to market dominance in America. Fred honored the work with a review, which is printed on the first page of the book. In honor of Fred, all net proceeds of the sales of *Stihl American* for the first year will be contributed to an educational endowment established in Fred's name at Old Dominion University. Fred's legacy, as well as that of STIHL's, will endure.

ENDNOTES

1   Waldemar Schafer, Stihl, Schaffer Poeschel, 2006, 1.

2   ———, 1.

3   ———, 48.

4   Tull-Williams, Advertisement, *Chain Saw Age*, October 1960.

5   S. H. Evans, "The Andreas Stihl Story," *Chain Saw Age*, August (1965), 31.

6   ———, 33.

CPSIA information can be obtained
at www.ICGtesting.com
Printed in the USA
BVOW03s2241201117

500360BV00013B/2/P